HOMESCHOOL
by design

A BEGINNERS GUIDE TO EDUCATING YOUR CHILDREN FROM HOME

Monica La Vella

Cold Rock Publishing

Canada

Monica La Vella/Cold Rock Publishing

Lincoln, Ontario, Canada

www.homeschoolbydesign.com

Homeschool By Design/Monica La Vella. —1st ed.

ISBN 978-1-988453-23-1

Contents

INTRODUCTION

Let's Get To Know Each Other
Characters in this book 1

GET ANCHORED ISLAND

Why Are We Here?
*The basics + the reasons that keep us
homeschooling*... 10

Rules To Follow...Designed Your Own Way
*The laws, rules, and expectations of home
schooling*.. 26

The Homeschool Audit
Observing for 24 hours............................ 34

METHOD ISLAND

Oh, The Ways You Can Teach!
Homeschool styles and methods............. 46

MECHANISM ISLAND

Plan Your Day...Or Not
All the ways to plan your days.................. 77

Documenting Learning
Simple steps to keep track of education... 98

i

ORGANIZATION ISLAND

Organizing Your Space
Plan for the place...................................... 111

Tools of the Trade
What you need.. 120

Homeschooling on a Budget
Get the most for your money...................... 128

ALL FOR YOU ISLAND

Self Love
Doing things for you..................................... 137

Work From Home and Homeschooling
You can do both... 152

Common Homeschool Questions
Let's get them answered............................. 159

NOW WHAT ISLAND

Where Do We Go From Here?
Disembarking from our journey................. 176

BONUS ISLAND

Crisis Schooling
Educating during a quarantine.................. 180

This book is dedicated to you, my readers. You are willing to go all in and move forward in this quest of the unknown and I honour you for that. If I could send you chocolate I would.

"When you change the way you look at things, the things you look at change."

—*Dr. Wayne Dyer*

He was a smart man, don't you think? When you change the way you *think* you should homeschool and design it how you *want* to, the concept changes. You make it yours.

Before we take to the Sea of Knowledge, be sure to download your field guide at www.HomeschoolByDesign.com.

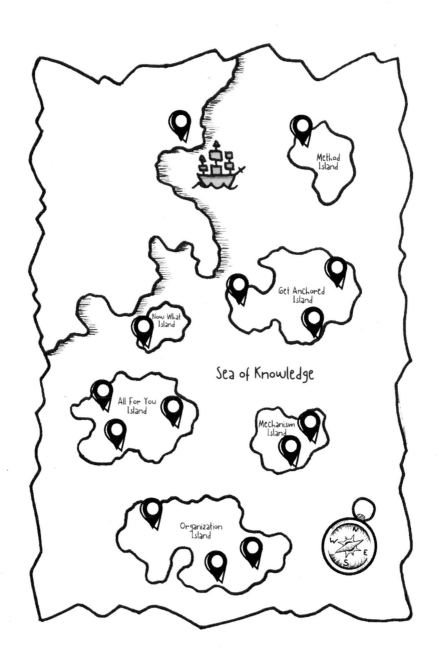

Characters in this book

WOULD YOU DEEM it inappropriate to have my book full of emojis and hearts? Because I'm the sort of gal that fills up her texts with those sorts of things and it's really hard to write a book without the expression of emoticons.

That's my design.

I welcome you to this book that will fill you with inquiries, contemplations, and probably a whole bunch of questions. That's a good thing! It means you've learned the basics and want to keep going. It means I've done what I've come to do, and that is to take you on a quest to set up your homeschool – perfectly designed for you.

The term Homeschool By Design came to me about a year before I considered this book a real possibility. My husband and I have believed profoundly in the phrase 'Life By Design' for years (and both have it tattooed on our bodies). We've arrived at the place we are in now based on this philosophy we've followed since we married in 2005. I quit my job at the school board and joined him in entrepreneurship because we had these big, hairy, audacious goals and believed hard in our dreams. Although it took a solid 13 years of not giving up, we hit them all.

This same phrase lent itself entirely to our homeschool life. That one can design their homeschool precisely as they wish seems to be a dream of so many rather than a goal that can be accomplished. Limiting beliefs hold us back (if I don't do it just like the school system, my child will end up on the streets). There are self-care habits we're missing (nope, drinking 5 cups of coffee doesn't count as self-care). There are judgements we fear ("What's that? You're homeschooling? You know your kid's going to turn out messed up, right?").

I'm here as a guide on this journey as you throw up your sails and take to the sea of knowledge. You'll have those fears and judgements walk the plank so you can move toward your goal – to design a homeschool that's right for you and your family. If that's not your goal, you may have grabbed the wrong book. #sorrynotsorry

Before we embark on the quest, let's get to know your guide a bit, shall we? That's me, by the way. Usually, this is saved for the end where you learn more about the author, but you don't want to take off on the ride of your life without knowing the person guiding you there, right? I'm not one to follow the rules, and this is my book by design {insert that winky emoji here}, so let's get into it.

I have loved working with my kids my entire life, first, as a babysitter, then a nanny for two summers. As a teen, I was a camp counsellor for 5 summers and went to university to become a teacher.

Between university and Teacher's College, I wanted to get experience in the school system and was offered a job as an educational resource worker for kindergarten to grade three. I went in with a heart full of love for students and such a fire to teach! I poured all of myself into my work, creating unique materials for my students and designing new strategies no one had ever considered. The head of the department even convinced me to sell my educational products online. I felt like I was in just the right place for me.

After three months, the principal called me in to do my 3-month review, and I'll *never* forget what she told me.

"Your enthusiasm will start affecting the students..."

Awesome – I thought – that's precisely what I was hoping to do! Light their sparks of interest and turn those sparks into flames of passion for learning!

"It's too much. You need to lessen your enthusiasm."

My heart dropped. How could my enthusiasm and excitement for educating be too much? Because it got the students excited to learn? Because they would shriek with joy when I sang action songs with them as they discovered a new concept?

Well, I figured she must be right – she *was* the principal. I was only twenty-two; what did I know? So I dimmed my light.

It took me only two years before I quit because it sucked the life out of me. I came home crying most days. I hated working in the school system. The joy of teaching left me so quickly. All the politics, the rules, the limitation on how to teach, the complying with 'standards.'

The system chewed me up and spat me out. I wasn't anywhere close to being strong enough to stand up for change. My soon-to-be husband and I decided right then and there that we would homeschool our future children.

Here were a few realizations I had about the school system that didn't sit well with me:

1. The education system as a whole is based upon meeting specific standards. It offers little room (if any) for what each individual child enjoys or expresses an interest in.
2. All children are expected to meet specific criteria at the same time.

3. Failure is feared instead of embraced. If we don't get good grades, we will get in trouble.
4. There are some exceptional teachers out there (I know many myself!), but the system fails them.

Before I go on, let's get one thing straight. I'm definitely not here to put down the education system. I'm sharing my experience because it's time some changes were made. I mean, this is the same system we've used in North America for hundreds of years...*hundreds*! Umm...a few things have changed since then. This isn't one of them. Why? How?

Who knows? The point is, you've picked up this book because there's likely something you've realized: you have different expectations of what education should look like, you're not happy with the way the system seems right now, you know you can do it better, or some reason between. My reasons were all of those.

It's my wish for you that you come out of this book on the side of 'hey, I can totally do this' and know you've got me cheering you on.

The Characters

Just like a fiction book, this one has characters. I'd like you to know them now, so you don't get confused as we go along.

To start, there's me. Homeschooling mama, who thinks she's pretty cool (although I think they now say 'lit'), even if my kids don't know so. I'm an early riser and lover of tea, vegan chocolate and EDM. I'm also a serial entrepreneur. Don't get me started on all the things I do.

There's my true love one and only, my husband Louie, who is a genius in the world of marketing music festivals and nightclubs. He's a night owl and thrives on chaos (especially in Las Vegas) and can be found speaking on podcasts and stages all over North America.

Next is my oldest, Avery, who is 11 at the time of this publishing. He's an inventor, an empath, an entrepreneur, a social butterfly, and has a giving and compassionate heart. He's also a Capricorn and can show off his raging, stubborn side sometimes, too. He'll make an incredible CEO of his own company one day.

Cruz is the youngest, three days from 10 the time of this publishing. He's the smartest kid I know. He was creating Instagram filters for Daddy's festival clients when he was only 8 years old. He's on the quieter side, an introverted and independent little guy. He's a lover of technology, an incredible coder, and an avid reader. He wants you to know he plans on being a famous YouTuber one day.

Where to now?

You are about to embark on a magical quest through various islands in the Sea of Knowledge. Fun, right? You'll be visiting islands with multiple destinations, gathering souvenirs, and will come out of your journey with a fully designed homeschool. Do you feel the excitement building up?

As on any journey, there are a few things you will need. The first is your satchel. This satchel will exist in your mind, and it will contain particular items you'll require on this quest. These items  will be revealed to you on the various islands you will visit and will be very useful to you as you create your homeschool by design.

The second item you'll need is your Field Guide, which can be found to download free on the Homeschool By Design website. You'll use this guide during every island visit to take notes, collect souvenirs, and design your homeschool as you go.

Third, you'll need to gather your highlighter and sticky notes because I'm giving you permission to mark this book up. That's it's purpose – to make it yours. Doodle in it put stars and hearts and stickers in your favourite spots, enjoy the read with a cup of tea – spill some on this book, even – and embrace this path.

There will be pirates to battle (careful of the comparison thief), obstacles to overcome (no letting aunt

Sally tell you you're crazy for choosing this path), and beliefs to build (you can do this).

You hold the map to your most significant treasure. The quest that will lead you from where you are now to the best homeschool design for your family. Let's visit our first island, **Get Anchored Island**.

Grab your satchel, your Field Guide, and your tools and hold onto the railing because it's going to be a wild adventure!

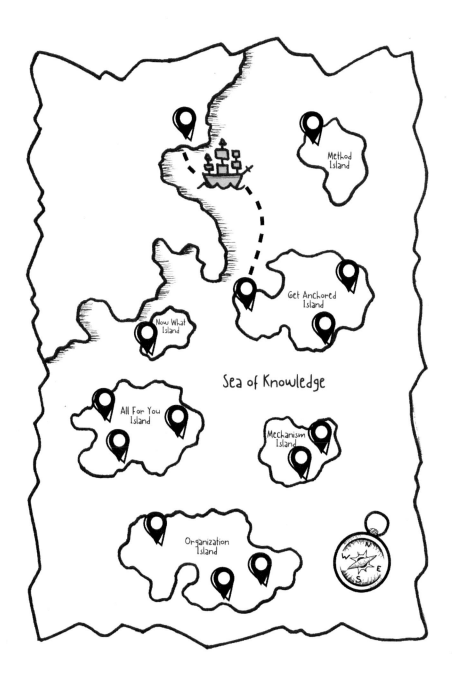

The basics + the reasons we keep on homeschooling

WE'VE ARRIVED ON **Get Anchored Island** and our first destination to visit: *Why Are We Here?* We're just going to dive in and start with one of the most asked questions by anyone considering the idea of home-schooling.

How do you start homeschooling?

I like to answer this by saying there's no one way to homeschool. It can be designed to look like whatever you want it to look like. It's the entire point of this book, right?

Some families feel calm when they have a schedule in place, similar to that of traditional schools. Other families feel calm without a set schedule and prefer to set a rhythm for their days. Others make no plans at all and design their days based on the interests of their children.

All of these are the best ways to homeschool because they fit each family best – Homeschool By Design.

So again, how do you start homeschooling? Here's the gist of it:

- Consider any local laws around homeschooling.
- Observe how your children learn best.
- Think about what kind of homeschooler you would like to be.
- Check out the various curriculum.
- Decide on what routine (or lack of one) will work best for you and your kids.

Are you sweating? It's not that complicated, I promise! This book will walk you through all the steps, so you have yourself a reliable place to start.

The Basics

Families choose to homeschool for a variety of reasons. For some, it's because they know they can do it better than a traditional school. For others, it's because they know their child would thrive better at home. Sometimes the choice is related to scheduling or traveling, or perhaps it's because the family wants to be the one to raise their children with the morals and values that are important to them.

There are many other reasons, but know this: each reason is reason enough to homeschool your child.

The comment I hear most often from people is, *"I could never homeschool my kids,"* followed by the laundry list of excuses people make about why they couldn't do it. If you are reading this book and wonder if you could ever homeschool, I tell you yes. Yes, you can.

The only thing you need is the small seed in your heart, the calling, the nudge, the voice that guides you, and suggested this crazy quest in the first place. That's all you need. The rest will fall into place.

The concept behind Homeschool By Design is to create an education unique to you and your family alone. It's not like Suzi down the street who grows all her own food or Becky on Instagram with her picture-perfect schoolroom. And if you are a version of Suzi or Becky, if that's your Homeschool By Design, then you do you.

Homeschool By Design isn't just one idea or one way to homeschool. It can be the ways and also none of the ways. It's the way that is yours and yours alone.

I've seen homeschools that are very strict and literally take school and do it at home (from the bell to recess and everything), and I've seen those free and open and follow only their passions. Is either of these right or wrong? They are only right for you if that's what you want your homeschool to look like. And they're only wrong for you if it's not what you want your home-school to look like. The choice is entirely yours. It's that simple. It's one of my favorite parts of homeschooling and something I wish I knew earlier on my journey.

***

One year I splurged on a history curriculum that came close to $500 and was meant to cover a couple of years worth of our country's history. It was beauti-ful and fun and arrived with a box filled with various materials – like stickers and washi tape – to use along with it. I was so excited to start!

I could picture it in my head: the boys coming downstairs and giving me a hug, telling me how happy they were about this new curriculum. Them learning all the things, joining some history club, and becoming historical writers. Or archeologists. Or some magical career path due to this curriculum.

When they came downstairs, the boys were less thrilled. The lessons didn't excite them, it was a lot of cut and paste, and the concepts weren't really sticking with them. They were doing the motions to 'get it over with' rather than to learn.

This was totally my fault.

I hadn't observed. I didn't listen. Their style of learning wasn't meant for cut-and-paste activities (which killed this crafty mama). I realized I had failed them in purchasing a curriculum that suited my inter-ests over their learning.

It wasn't a total waste, though, since there were all sorts of video links and articles to read along with it. That's the sort of stuff they liked. As it turns out, I got to keep all the stickers and washi tape to myself. #momforthewin

***

The beauty of Homeschool By Design is that you can try something out with your kids for one day, one month, or one year. If it doesn't work out to their/ your liking, you switch it up again. It's all about trial and error, finding out what works best for their learning styles, and finding out what keeps you enjoying the process as an educator.

<u>Why Do You Choose To Homeschool?</u>

There's a book called "Start With Why" by Simon Sinek (he also has a few TED Talks I highly recommend), and he writes about discovering the core reasons we do what we do. It's that reason – or your *why* – that will govern your decisions.

For example, if you homeschool so your family can travel, then all your decisions will be wrapped around traveling. You may decide not to sign your kids up for activities at the local homeschool coop because of your travel plans.

If your why is so you can allow your children the freedom to dive deeper into a topic of their interest, you'll keep an open schedule for free time.

To go a bit deeper into this, if you homeschool so you can travel, why is that important? Why is it important to you and your family to travel? Perhaps it's so your children can be immersed in various cultures. Well then, why is *that* important? Maybe it's because your vision for your children is to be wildly diverse and traveled so they may have opportunities as adults. *That* is a strong why. That is something that will drive your desire to homeschool when the going gets tough.

I challenge you to get clear about your *why*. When your *why* is strong and unshakable, there's no turning back. You're in this for the long haul. Even your aunt's friend's cousin, who tells you of the kid she knew in school who was homeschooled and was so weird, won't get you down. No sir-ey. No child's defiance and no in-laws questioning about your decision can make you waver from this homeschooling journey.

When you are so strongly confident in your *why* nothing will shake you, your *why* is your North Star. Your *why* will determine your path.

For example, let's say Sara wants to homeschool because she feels like her daughter would thrive better at home. That is important to her because she wants her daughter to have the best chance in life. *That* is important because Sara sees a lot of potential in her daughter and knows she has so much to offer the world. Her *why* for homeschooling is because she knows her daughter has so much to offer the world, and it will best express itself through home learning.

Let's come up with yours. Here are a few questions to guide you. Refer to your Field Guide to take notes.

List all the reasons you want to homeschool.

_____

_____

_____

_____

_____

Out of the list, what is the most important reason for you to homeschool?

_____

Why is that reason important?

_____

_____

And why is THAT important (see example above for what I'm trying to get you to do here)?

_____

_____

So early in our quest, and I'm already putting you to work! Stick with it, though, because we are carving out the foundation for your Homeschool By Design. These answers are shaping how the rest of this journey will play out.

What type of character traits do you want your children to have?

_____

_____

What vision do you want to create for your home-school? Use your senses. How does it feel and sound? What does it look like?

_____

_____

And let's get even deeper, just a few more questions, I promise!

If you named your homeschool, what would it be called (e.g., you could try using something like "*Your Street Name* Academy," but, really, anything goes)?

_____

Write out a mission statement for your home-school. This could include parts of your why, the vision for what you want to create in your homeschool, morals and values you want to focus on, etc.

Our mission at _____
(homeschool name) is _____

_____
_____(you can touch on your why here) so
our children _____
_____ (explain
what you want for your children based on your why)

If you're feeling stuck, here's an example of our mission statement: *Our mission at Meadow Wood Academy is to encourage self-led learning so our children can focus on their strengths and passions, leading them to greatness in their desired fields of study.*

This is our North Star. This is the item in my mind's satchel I keep close. I can take this mission statement on a rough day and remind myself why I haven't sent them to school yet. It'll pick me back up off the bathroom floor where I'm eating chocolate. I love my why.

I want you to think of your child as a coconut (aww...so cute!). They are these round seeds that fit into the palm of our hands, yet have the potential stirring inside to grow into an enormous palm tree. All they need is soil, sun, and water.

You are holding your child's education in the palm of your hand. You have the resources to nurture their creativity, dreams, and imaginations. It's all right here. The answers to those questions are the planting of the seeds of education.

<u>Why Homeschool? Why Now?</u>

Homeschooling has never been easier. We live in a world where we no longer need to memorize our multiplication tables because the answer is in your back pocket (you know: your phone). Instead, we can dive into topics much deeper, and that light us up.

I've mentioned that Cruz is an incredible coder. He saved up all his birthday and Christmas money one year and bought himself his first laptop when he was six. Six, you guys! And he did that because he wanted to code on his own computer and not rely on mine or Daddy's. He wanted to dive deeper into his learning without the restrictions of using our laptops.

Over these years, I've never had my kids sit down and memorize their math facts, and this is why: they will never, ever be without technology to do it for them. The formulas they can memorize (we know in this house that area = base times height), but the facts they don't. The days of memorization are over – the age of information is here.

This will ruffle a lot of feathers, I know. I was once that mama who swore up and down that my kids would never have screens. Avery went almost 2 years before we let him even watch TV. What changed my mind was understanding their future. Unless there's some kind of zombie apocalypse (and if there is, no math memorization will help anyways), we will forever have facts at our fingertips through our phones and any other future device our children will have. Or invent.

This was the beginning of my Homeschool By Design. I realized that, although the curriculum was still telling me to get my kids to memorize, them remembering facts would not get them to their goals any faster. Although this may not be everyone's design for their children's education, this is mine. And mine isn't the right way, it's just our way. Almost everyone else I know sticks to the curriculum. They have their kids memorize. It's just not for my kids or me.

If it's your thing, then own it! Get your kids in those spelling bees and blow people's minds with how incredible they can remember the word *insouciant* (I literally Googled 'spelling bee words' to complete that sentence). That might be your Homeschool By Design, and that's awesome! But if it isn't, know that I've got your back when the curriculum or school system tell you otherwise.

All The Free Things

I'll repeat it: there has never been an easier time to educate your kids from home. Even for families with both parents working, there are so many work-from-home opportunities out there. It's totally do-able to work around shifts and homeschool (we will get to this on **All For Your Island**).

It's also the greatest time in history to be alive. We have copious amounts of free information via internet searches and YouTube you can literally teach yourself – and your children – everything: from how to do your makeup to how to do your taxes.

I used YouTube tutorials to publish my first three children's books. I didn't need to wait for a publisher to pick it up; I did it myself. I also used YouTube to teach myself how to teach math, understand gender pronouns, and make tonight's dinner. The list is unending.

***

When I came out with my third children's book, my kids understood what it meant to be an author; they wanted to be authors, too. We spent a few weeks on the first step of publishing, which is the first draft.

As a kid in school, I remember my first drafts having only red pen marks for corrections. I was taught those first drafts should be clean and coherent, so I didn't have to re-write everything, only a couple of mi-

nor mistakes. I was taught it should make sense and be complete from beginning to end.

It turns out this isn't how to write a story at all.

Watch a few YouTube videos from writing coaches or best-selling authors, and you'll find out that the first draft is like getting all of your ideas out of your head and onto paper, or your preferred version of technology. They are meant to be messy. They are full of mistakes and holes.

This book is a perfect example of that. I didn't even include this story until the second draft when I began piecing all my random thoughts into topics and topics into chapters.

For my boys, I've come to embrace the messiness of the first draft. I've stopped myself from reminding them about punctuation and capital letters at the beginning of a sentence even though my eye twitches a bit when my type-A personality sees the sight of a run-on sentence.

After that first draft, they're able to piece things together easily and enjoy finding their own mis-spelling and punctuation.

They love to draw out designs for book covers, and once we even published each of their books. It cost us less than $5.00 for them to print and have it in their hands. What an experience! All based on the free learning of book publishing available online.

***

Homeschooling is drawing more families because of its flexibility. Taking from the story above, when my boys were inspired to write, they would do it at bedtime. I swear it was because they knew I wouldn't force them to bed. And why would I? They were writing!

They'd sit on the floor of my room with papers all over, and markers lined up, writing and drawing out their ideas and storylines. They picked it up again whenever they felt like writing. There wasn't a specific writing time where they were forced to sit down and write a story; it came as it did. When inspired, they wrote. When not inspired, we did grammar lessons.

Cruz with his published book

How do I know I'm doing it right?

I remember when Avery was learning how to walk. It was so exciting to watch him over those months of growth. I noticed how he developed so many different parts that all had to fit together to allow his legs to move in a way that would let him walk. It started when he was only three months old – learning to hold his head up all by himself. It was the first of many developments that led to his walking, and I didn't even realize it until I looked back. After months of tummy time, he could start to roll over. We would clap and squeal with delight with those first rolls! From there, he started sitting up, developing his core muscles, keeping balance, and not just falling over.

Eventually, he became curious. He started crawling around and then pulling himself up on the couch and learning how to balance these two wobbly legs. Weeks went by. His muscles grew stronger. Soon he went from slowly moving along the couches to being very swift and even standing on his own.

And then, it happened.

I was about to go out and meet some moms in my mom group when Avery took his first step. I was overjoyed! We were thrilled to see our baby boy take his first steps!

Looking back on all of this, I can see he didn't just take his first step. He took all the lessons he had learned over the months of his new life, all the muscles he had trained and strengthened, all the connections he made in his brain, and put them together to make that first step happen.

You are a new homeschooler. You're not going to get it all at once, and you need to give yourself some grace. Remember: you are new to this world of home-schooling, just like Avery was new to the world. He didn't come out walking, and you will not come into this knowing exactly what to do or how to do it. That's the beauty of it. There is no way of knowing how to do it right or if you're doing it right. It becomes right as you try things out, test things out, and learn what works and what doesn't for yourself and your children.

Are you sick of it yet? Because I'm going to keep saying it. There is no right way to homeschool. There is only your way to homeschool, and that is unique to you and your family.

Benefits of Homeschool By Design

Let's list a few reasons why designing your homeschool for you and your family is such an excellent idea:

1. You don't compare yourself to anyone else because you're doing it your own way.
2. You can be proud to tell any nay-sayers that it doesn't look like school because it's not supposed to.
3. Your sanity is saved by lessening the intensity of high expectations.
4. Homeschool can happen at any time and any day.

Sounds pretty great, right? Now that I have you convinced, let's head over to our next destination.

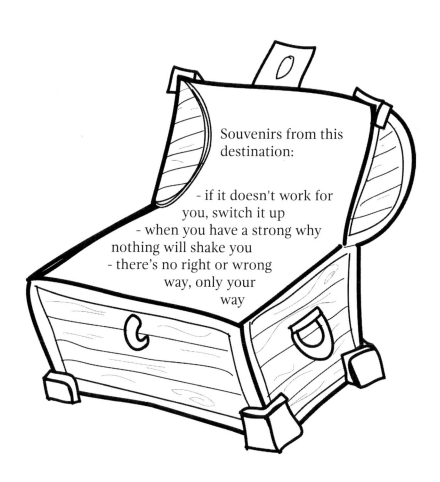

Souvenirs from this destination:

- if it doesn't work for you, switch it up
- when you have a strong why nothing will shake you
- there's no right or wrong way, only your way

The laws, rules, and expectations of homeschooling

WE'VE HIT AN obstacle at our next destination. Those are the rules. Here's the part where you either roll your eyes at the consideration of such a thing or celebrate with joy because you have something to follow. Either way, you need to get to know the laws that govern the place you live in. And sometimes, those laws can really feel like obstacles.

The rules and laws of homeschool vary greatly: from strict documenting and outlining every lesson plan for every subject to no regulations at all.

We fall into the 'no rules at all' category unless your child has attended the public school system. If this is the case, parents are required to submit a 'Letter of Intent' every year to the school board to notify them of their choice to homeschool. Since we never registered our boys to enter into school, this isn't something we've ever done.

Here's a list of the most restrictive US states:

Massachusetts
New York
Rhode Island
Pennsylvania
Vermont

Here's a list of the least restrictive US states:

Alaska
Connecticut
Idaho
Illinois
Indiana
Iowa
Michigan
Missouri
New Jersey
Oklahoma
Texas

I know you just got started on this chapter, but let's pause for a quick second and look up 'homeschooling laws for *your state or province*.'

What comes up? Mark it down in your Field Guide.

If you're in a more restrictive area, you may feel like this obstacle just got a whole lot bigger. Have no fear! You've got something special hiding in your satchel. Reach in there and pull out the Accepting Goggles. These will help you see things (like rules) in a more accepting way.

For instance, if you are required to send in a Letter of Intent, it's as simple as downloading a template (there are tons of options online), filling it out, and sending it in. Then you use the same one each year. We can accept this because it's super simple and requires less than 5 minutes each year.

The Accepting Goggles will also move you through this obstacle much faster. The longer you sit in the pity party, the more likely you'll be left behind on this island. Accept what you need to do and move on! No time for complaining or excuses when we've got a homeschool to design.

Now, if you find you're struggling to *understand* the rules, you have nothing in your satchel for that. What you do have is support. Go online and find groups in your region. You'll often find other mamas happy to help you navigate through this part. Take it step-by-step and know thousands have come down this path before you and will take your hand as you navigate your way through.

Requirements for Homeschooling

Even though this varies across so many areas, let's look at some requirements you may find.

Letter of Intent – As I mentioned above, this is the only requirement in our province. This yearly letter notifies the school board or superintendent on your plans to homeschool your child. This simple letter is a quick task to complete. Templates for these letters can be found online and cover what you need to include for your specific area. Embrace this task; otherwise, they'd be calling out Johnny's name on the first day of school attendance list and wonder if he's lost or something.

Attendance – Tracking attendance means you track the days your child is learning (Hello? Every day!) and note any sick days, vacation days, etc. Some areas also require you to indicate the number of hours your children receive instruction. Again, this is simple to track.

Standardized Testing – You may live in an area that requires standardized testing, the same testing public school students would receive. Your local education authorities will tell you how and when these will take place.

Portfolio – These often include samples of work done from each subject over the year, medical records, standardized test results, photos of more significant projects, etc. Even if this isn't a requirement for you, I highly suggest keeping one just for fun! More on that later.

Instruction Plan – Just as most homeschoolers do anyway, the instruction plan covers the various topics or concepts planned for the upcoming year.

Okay, take a breath! It's not all that bad. It may seem overwhelming if you've never done it before, but these things don't take long and are pretty simple.

If you're freaking out al little bit, why don't we dig into your satchel and see what other tools we have? Here it is! Affirmations. Try taking another breath and repeat after me...'I follow what is required because it is a part of my Homeschool By Design.' And now release it.

You've got this.

Expectations for Learning

Whether you're purchasing an online curriculum or putting things together yourself, you've probably asked yourself how to know what your kids are expected to know. It's a really simple one to discover, too!

With a quick internet search, you can have the curriculum expectations in your hand in less than 5 minutes. Simple search '_____ (your state/ province) curriculum expectations' and you'll quickly find the standards for your area. Pop the results of your search in your Field Guide.

These documents are usually in PDF form and can be printed based on the grade or subject.

***

Kindergarten meant we were officially going against the grain. We were finally considered true homeschoolers. We were rebels! Despite feeling quite rebellious, I still wanted to keep as close to the school expectations as possible.

After finding the PDF document on the expectations for our area, I printed it off (all 90-something pages), hole punched the paper, and carefully placed it in my new teacher binder. I was ready to go!

My big plan was to go through the document and highlight each expectation as we went through them. This lasted about 5 seconds. It was way too complicated. Instead, I used the expectations in my documenting.

For example, one expectation for kindergarten was: "collect, organize, display, and interpret data to solve problems and to communicate information, and explore the concept of probability in everyday contexts."

Honestly, this sounds like an expectation for my accountant.

The boys had graphs they completed daily where they selected whether it was sunny, cloudy, rainy, or snowy. I took that fancy-worded expectation and documented the observations we made from weather patterns over the fall and winter. Simple. Done. That expectation was complete.

***

If you want to follow what I did, you can print out your region's expectations and design your lessons around curriculum expectations or just purchase a curriculum for their age group and throw expectations out the window. I used the technique in the story until grade two. After that point, I realized I could freely design my homeschool. Following the curriculum, expectations were no longer something in my design. We adjusted and took another path.

Getting Help

The thought of your child's entire education being in the palm of your hand may give you the deer-in-the-headlights sort of look. It's a lot to take on. Checking into the homeschool laws for you may put your mind at ease. Here's why.

You don't have to be the only one teaching your children.

Whew! Feels much better, right? Again, check into the laws in your location, but for most, nothing is wrong with hiring things out! Some families hire a tutor to come and teach their children the curriculum. Others might sign their children up for online classes.

There are so many great co-ops out there to join, or you could do an exchange with a homeschooling friend who's Spanish speaking, and you love art.

This is another way to Homeschool By Design. It takes a village, as they say, and it's the truth. You're not in this thing alone.

Being Organized

In following specific laws, this is where heightened organization comes into play. Some areas require home visits to ensure education is on track. You want to keep all your ducks in a line without being consumed by the idea of a lady coming to your house and taking your kids away because you forgot to teach decimals. (PS, it doesn't work that way).

If you're not an organizer, your heart might be palpitating right now. Umm...organizing? But listen, we'll be visiting another island a little later where I make this really simple and laid out.

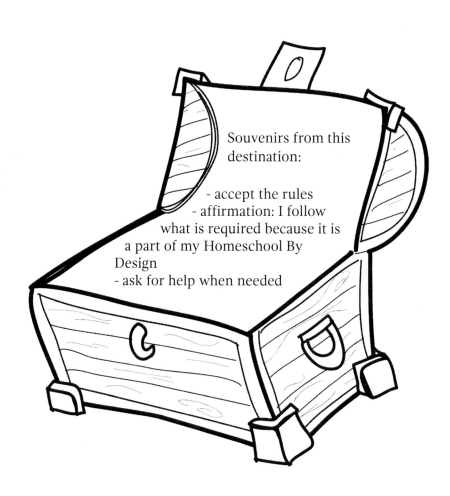

Souvenirs from this destination:

- accept the rules
- affirmation: I follow what is required because it is a part of my Homeschool By Design
- ask for help when needed

Observing for 24 hours

THIS IS ONE of my favorite destinations because you will learn a simple technique that will save your homeschool again and again.

When the children were entering school age, I read about a homeschool audit. That is, taking note of the questions they ask, the TV shows they watch, the games they play, their reactions to their siblings, the activities they want to learn, and anything else that goes on within 24 hours.

Brilliant! I thought.

I purchased a special journal (which is what I do as soon as I see a new idea for something...I swear I have a hundred scattered throughout my house) and noted all the things. We were on a road trip to Nova Scotia, so this type of documenting was easy to do. We sat in a car all day, and our children were full of questions.

My journal quickly filled with sticky notes of questions, thoughtful ideas, and funny quotes the kids said. They wanted to learn math with donuts and find out where exactly a lobster lived in the ocean. So many ideas to focus on!

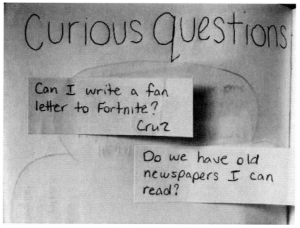

Some questions they asked and I kept in my journal.

With this homeschool audit, I was able to hone in on their curiosities and make a plan moving forward. I took their thoughts and used them to design our homeschool in a way that worked for the boys. I bravely threw curriculum options out the window and followed what my heart desired and theirs.

A homeschool audit can happen in a few different ways.

- It can be a way to reflect where you are and design a plan for where you want to go
- It can be a way to recognize holes in your children's learning or as a way for you to discover what they want to learn
- It answers that question: how do I know what my children love most?

Why You Should Do a Homeschool Audit

There is a whole host of varied reasons to audit your homeschool. From new homeschoolers to veteran homeschoolers, we can all use an audit. To this day, I still audit our homeschool when something doesn't feel right, and we need to switch things up.

For you, as a newbie-homeschooler, this is one of the greatest gifts. It will be the key to understanding your children, their thought processes, and their passions! And I mean really understanding. We hear our kids all day long, sure, but we don't *hear* them, you know?

I mean, there's only so much talk of Minecraft one can have before you've completely tuned out.

Being present with a pencil and journal during these conversations leads to ah-ha moments. For example, you might hear something like:

"I built a wooden pickaxe and dug down and got stone to build a stone pickaxe and then mined iron for an iron pickaxe, and then I found diamonds!"

Huh?

Right. We've all had those conversations where we had no clue what they were talking about but still smiled and nodded. This is actually a gift!

Check your satchel for your Learning Lens. If you pick apart that sentence and put on your Learning Lens, you will see *precisely* what kind of a gift this is.

Your child just spoke about geology. They knew what they had to do if they wanted to find diamonds. They had to build a certain pickaxe. To construct a pickaxe, one needs a crafting table to put together the item. Once it's built, they can mine – all sorts of learning here already.

They follow up with a question:

"How do I find diamonds in real life?"

Ah-ha! There it is, mama! The question you note in your journal. They have been playing Minecraft and are trying to make the concept relatable in their real, actual life.

Under normal circumstances, you might answer *They come from diamond mines*' and leave it at that. But we are in homeschool audit mode.

With your Learner Lenses on, you can take this to the next level. You could have them:

- watch a video on mining for diamonds
- map out diamond mines around the world
- list the ways diamonds are used (not just jewelry!)
- learn about the process and timeline of the creation of diamonds
- understand the karat measurement
- draw a picture of a Minecraft diamond and real diamond to compare
- explore the technology used to harvest diamonds

Their passion can start a whole slew of added learning opportunities! And guess what? The above suggestions cover quite a few subjects: geography, history, writing, math, science, and art. You could even throw in gym class by digging a hole in the backyard to see what they find.

By being excited to learn these things with your child, you're showing them that their interests are important. You are being a mentor, offering resources and ideas for the projects most important to them.

The way you find out what's most important is through a homeschool audit.

Just don't wear your Learning Lenses forever. Eventually, you might hear what I often do, "Mom, does EVERYTHING have to be about learning?". I'm sure I'll take mine off someday.

When to Complete an Audit

Once you start your homeschooling adventure, you will find you want to do audits at different times. You may want to do a yearly audit before starting a new school year or calendar year. Here, you could do an overview of what's coming up and check in with each child. Discover where their current interests lie and add those into your planning.

You may end up in a rut during the homeschool year and want to switch things up. This is an excellent time for an audit!

If things are feeling unbalanced or when everyone seems unhappy and dragging and want to switch gears, a new focus audit could come to the rescue!

***

One November, I felt like we had hit a bit of a rut. We were used to our curriculum, and the newness of the year had faded. The days were getting darker, and I felt like we needed to switch things up a bit or add something exciting.

I did a homeschool audit and noticed how much the boys enjoyed poetry. Mainly, creating funny rhyming phras-

es about poop (which to the untrained eye wouldn't seem like poetry at all). I used this interest in our homeschool, and that's where I found Julie Bogart and her Poetry Tea Time concept (you must visit her site). The idea behind poetry tea time is to enjoy poetry with yummy drinks and snacks in a special atmosphere.

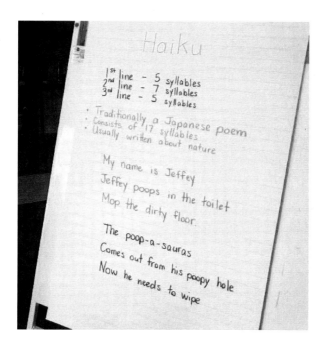

I took the kids to a local thrift shop where they selected their very own teacups. By some miracle, we also found a mini quilt with an entire tea theme to it! It was four bucks.

We decided Tuesdays would be our poetry tea time dates. We baked cookies, then made tea and collected our poetry books. We set the table with our tea quilt and laid the cups at each spot. We took turns reading silly poetry as we drank our tea and nibble on our cookies. It lasted maybe 15 minutes, and it was the best!

After a couple of weeks, we invited the schooled neighborhood kids, and they decided they wanted to be in-

vited weekly. What started with a couple of poetry books, turned into many poetry books! I went with it. I watched as all the kids, especially Cruz, who was pretty shy at the time, came out of their shells and read in front of each other and laughed at the words they didn't understand and just enjoyed each other's company. I enjoyed it, too. It made me feel like I was my 5th-grade self and finally fit in (boohoo, I know, I was one of those kids).

This was all because I did an audit. I observed what the boys were drawn to and brought that forward into our days.

Poetry tea time lasted a couple of months until passion waned, and we moved on. I could have kept going, but what would be the point? They received what they needed from those fun, dark afternoons – whether it was writing or finding as many words as they could that rhymed with poop. I documented those days well so we can still look back and laugh at the memories. And I bet they'll want to bring it back to our days when winter comes again.

***

How to Do an Audit

Completing an audit is a simple process completed over one to two days. You document the various items, such as:

- questions your child asks
- the things they do
- what they listen to or watch
- requests they make
- routine they follow

I use a variety of materials to complete an audit, although not all at the same time. Sometimes I use a journal, other times sticky notes, and other times a worksheet. I've included one in your Field Guide if this is your preferred method of auditing.

As the day goes on and you mark these things down, you'll notice clues in their choices, questions, and behaviors.

Our kids leave us clues about who they really are and who they are here to be in this world. If you sit, pay attention, take notes, and document, you'll understand your children so much more than you realize.

What do they love to do when left to their own devices?

If you pulled away everything else and just toss them in the backyard, what would they do?

***

As a child, I left a lot of clues about who I would become. I'm a huge animal lover, and it wasn't very hard for my parents to see that. On camping trips, I would sit for up to an hour outside the trailer with seeds waiting for birds to trust me enough to land and eat them out of my palm. I would talk to them and let them know that I was trustworthy, and then it was OK to come and have a little snack. I believed I could communicate with them, and even to this day, you'll find me greeting birds on a walk. It's no surprise that I founded one of the biggest vegan food festivals in Canada.

As a pre-teen, my sister, my cousin, and I created our own businesses as a form of play. My dad would drive us all to the craft shop (on his lunch break...wasn't he the best?), and we would take our hard-earned money, and we would spend it on beads. We would then create jewelry, and we would sell them at the end of our driveway. No one ever came, but we came up with a sweet motto that we'd scream down the road: 'Don't be shy, come and buy!'

My dad was a general manager at a car dealership, and he would often bring back unused contracts and binders filled with various car color options. My sister, my cousin and I would play General Manager. We would sell cars to imaginary people, and we would convince them why they needed to buy them. We were little entrepreneurs. Looking at all three of us today, we are still entrepreneurs, and all run very successful businesses.

As a thirteen-year-old, I was obsessed with teaching. When I started babysitting, I would bring a big suitcase filled with educational activities and crafts for the children I would be looking after. This eventually led to my becoming a nanny, a camp counselor, and then going to school to teach.

I can't quite get away from that passion for teaching as I sit here and write this book with my hope you learn something that would help you on this path.

As you can see, there are many clues I left throughout my childhood about the person I would become.

***

All the memories that are most important and that I hold close ring true to who I am today. Our children are the same.

Can you imagine if my parents kept audits of my interests? Can you imagine if I had a mentor in my life to guide me to get deeper into my learning of being an entrepreneur?   Eventually, I figured it out myself, but it surely would have saved a lot of university tuition and time if I had followed my various interests beyond what seems to be 'play.'

Think about this for your child right now.

- What are they most passionate about?

- If you ask them what they want to learn about what they answer?
- How do they play?
- What tools do they use when they play?
- Are they crafty?
- Are they technologically driven?
- Do they love to play alone or with others?

Follow the path they are hinting to you through your audit and maybe take notes about your thoughts and where you see them in the future. In 15 or 20 years, wouldn't it be so fun to look back on this audit? You could gift it to your children, wrapped up in a pretty frame, as proof of their authenticity. Maybe I'm going a bit far, but you get my point.

What to Do with your Audit

The clues you find in your audit will leave you with a few options.

1. You can use your observations to choose a new topic for learning.
2. You can supply them with resources and tools to follow their interests (e.g., if a child loves horses, you may offer them an online course on caring for horses, buy them a horse coloring book, sign them up for horse riding lessons, etc.).
3. Choose or add a curriculum based on their current passions.
4. Practice strewing (that is, leaving items, books, or activities of interest out where your children will find them in hopes they will seek the knowledge themselves).

You'll know your audit is complete when you have a list of ideas, topics, subtopics, passions, and interests to refer to.

That's it for this island, homeschoolers! Make notes of your biggest ah-ha moments, takeaways, and souvenirs in your Field Guide, and let's move on to **Method Island**.

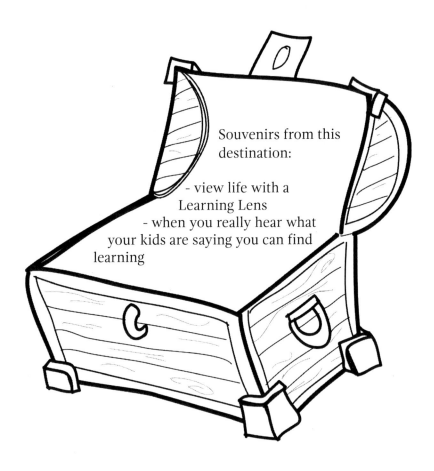

Souvenirs from this destination:

- view life with a Learning Lens
- when you really hear what your kids are saying you can find learning

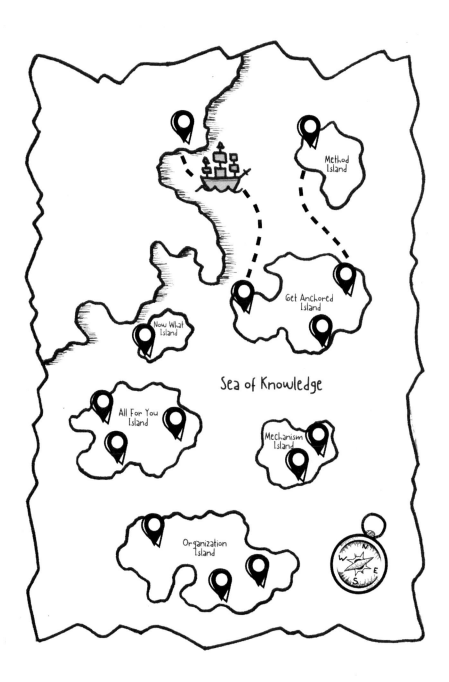

Homeschool styles and methods

ADVENTURE AWAITS! As we journey into the Sea of Knowledge to visit the next island, let's talk about one of the myths about homeschooling: that you are meant to turn your home into school. The truth is you actually have a choice.

Entering the homeschooling realm can seem very overwhelming when you realize that there's not just one method. There isn't one single curriculum we all follow. And there shouldn't be! All our kids are different and deserve an education that fits them the same way we, as adults, get a career path that suits us.

Instead of bringing school into the home, think of it as being educated at home. As the educator, you can make this process look however you want it to look. It could mean snuggling on the couch to read a book and baking cookies because the characters in the book baked cookies.

It could mean going to play in the river near your house for an entire day, noticing all the little minnows and frogs and rock formations, and how the current runs swiftly.

Homeschooling does not need to look like children sitting at a table for hours a day being forced to do worksheets. Unless, of course, that works for them. Then go bananas – that is your Homeschool By Design!

Having been educated in the school system and then working in the school system, it was the only model I knew when we began homeschooling. Want to know how I taught my boys? Exactly how they would have been taught at school.

I chose this route because *I thought* that was the only way my children could learn. It's all I knew. If the government had this big plan to educate kids, who was I to do it any differently?

Well, my heart desired different. But my head kept fighting that desire.

A couple of years into homeschooling, my heart won. I *really* did not want to teach my children as a reflection of the school system. I didn't want them memorizing facts and being dragged through task after task, especially when things like the arts were being taken away and out of schools.

I wanted to bring the arts into our learning.

I wanted my children to know facts because they cared about the facts, not because I had to memorize them from a test.

If my kids want to know the exact day World War II started, they'll ask Siri! What I *do* want them to know are the stories of their great-grandfather leading tanks through Italy and helping to protect Rome from being taken over by the Nazis. How he stayed behind in the Netherlands to help rebuild that nation while their great-grandmother waited at home in Canada, nursing to the sick and injured. That's what I want them to know and remember. That's the design I want for our homeschool.

Your design could be totally different. There is no right or wrong way to do this. Well, I guess there is a wrong way to do this, but you don't seem like the neglectful type.

You have children you love, so you will be doing what is best for them, no matter what. No one can tell you what education or learning looks like for your child, only you can. You know them best.

Methods to the Madness

We've arrived at our next port: **Method Island**.

There are various methods to homeschooling – betcha didn't realize that! I will outline them within the next few sections. Get your Field Guide ready, because this island is a doozy.

You might notice you find more than one method enticing, and that's good! Who doesn't love variety? You'll find reasons why each particular method may fit you best. Take the pieces of each method you are drawn to and include those in your Homeschool By Design.

Let's review your why and your mission statement before we fully immerse ourselves in this island filled with homeschool methods. Remember them. Then as you travel through these next few pages, mark off the styles you think will fit best with your design.

Things to consider:
- How long do you plan to homeschool? Is it open-ended?
- Are you looking for a curriculum-in-a-box type style, or do you prefer to go with the flow?
- Do you prefer a set routine, or do you prefer flexibility in your days?
- Is there a specific goal you have for educating your children at home?
- Are there any circumstances that can affect your decision to homeschool (e.g., finances, personal or medical issues)?

Complete the Field Guide worksheet to determine your style. Now grab your satchel and look for the sorting calculator – sort of like the Sorting Hat from Harry Potter – and continue through this section, sorting through the pieces that fit best for your family.

Traditional Homeschooling

This is the method most homeschoolers begin with because it is the method most familiar, having been in school before. Traditional homeschooling is doing school at home. Lessons start at the same time each day and finish at the same time each day, just like traditional schools. The day is structured around the various subjects, there's a use of tests and quizzes to track the progress of the children, and it has an end goal of preparing the child for post-secondary education. Traditional homeschooling offers a rigid structure that new homeschoolers often feel is needed and helps them feel at peace because they know they are following conventional school methods. It's excellent for children who thrive with a set structure or who have been recently pulled from school and wish to follow the same routine.

A Typical Day

A typical day for a traditional homeschooler can look like this:

9:00 am – Gather together to start lessons in language arts with each child receiving one-on-one help

9:30 am – Math lessons for each child, individual support as needed

10:00 am – Free time for younger children while older ones complete history

10:30 am – Snack for all, then clean up and read from a chapter book for all the kids

11:00 am – Social studies for all, then independent reading

12:00 pm – Lunch, clean up, play outside

1:00 pm – Science experiment with all kids, follow up activity separately based on level

1:45 pm – Quiet time for younger kids while older ones complete added lessons

2:30 pm – Complete the school day

Is It For You?

How to know if traditional homeschooling is for you:
* You and your children prefer structure
* You want to follow something familiar with your own experience
* You want to include tests, quizzes, and other traditional assessments
* You feel more confident with something familiar to you

- You plan to send your children back to school and want to keep the same routine

Unschooling

Although there are differing intensities, un-schooling is basically an informal learning method that encourages learning to be led by the children and their interests. This method is very relaxed and believes that with the natural curiosity in children, they will follow their own interests.

Not that they won't ever use a curriculum. For example, if Jeffey wants to learn about rocks, you can bet mom will find any resource she can so he can spend the time he wants to dive all in.

A Typical Day

A typical day for an unschooler doesn't really exist. They can all be so different depending on the family, the children, and their varying interests. Here's an example:

Morning: Get up at some point. One child makes every-one breakfast. He saw a recipe the kids made on Masterchef and wants to recreate it for everyone. His knife skills have really started to come along.

Mid-morning: One child heads outside to water the seedlings she transplanted into the garden. She brings her homemade journal out with her to take notes on how tall they grew. She searches for pests and talks to the plants like they are friends. She draws a picture of one of her tallest plants and names it Harry.
One child turns on the TV to play on his Xbox. There's a tournament he's been practicing for, and he meets his

friends online to practice before entering. Leadership abounds, they have a strategy in place, and they keep track of their stats as they begin the tournament.
One kid isn't feeling well and is stuck to mom's leg. He wants to snuggle and be read to.

After lunch: Walk to the local ice cream shop for a treat. Everyone brings their own money, the oldest helping the youngest reach the counter so he can pay.

Avery tinkering with a handheld video game.

Is It For You?

How to know if unschooling is for you:
- You prefer to go with the flow
- You believe children learn best by following their passions or interests
- You are comfortable documenting their progress by journaling, taking photos, or making notes

- You are open to allowing full trust in your child to know what they need to learn
- You prefer minimal structure so children can choose their best path of learning
- You have children with various learning styles
- You are comfortable being more of a mentor role in providing your children with resources they need for their different interests/projects (e.g., materials, books, articles, etc.)
- You are open to using anything as a learning opportunity, even poop...yes, you could learn about poop for days
- You believe children will learn what they need to learn on their own time
- You are open and willing to take the extra time finding resources to fulfill the interest of your children

Relaxed Homeschooling

Like unschooling, a relaxed homeschooler believes in the partnership between a parent and child in the learning. Still, they also believe that specific knowledge should be taught in the home.

As a relaxed homeschooler, one may incorporate some light curriculum while still allowing for plenty of child-led learning. It's a broad term, though, and you can find both traditional-type relaxed homeschoolers and unschooling-type relaxed homeschoolers. Do you know why? Because of Homeschool By Design, my friends. You can make any method look like your own.

A Typical Day

A typical day for a relaxed homeschooler can look like this:
9 am-ish: Kids come together to make breakfast

9:30 am: YouTube for movement/exercise
9:50 am: Online math games for each child
10:15 am: Online writing games for each child
10:45 am: Snack
11:00 am: Science experiment, history lesson, or geography, based on their current interests, for all children together
11:30 am: Snuggle up for read-aloud of a chapter book
12:00 pm: Make lunch
12:45 pm: Self-led learning for each child for the remaining of the day

Is It For You?

How to know if relaxed homeschooling is for you:
- You prefer a relaxed setting at home
- You believe children learn best by following their passions or interests, but still want to provide basic knowledge
- You want to have a set structure of learning for your children while still allowing for freedom of choice
- You are comfortable documenting their progress by journaling, taking photos, or making notes
- You have children with various learning styles
- You are comfortable being more of a mentor role in providing your children with resources they need for their different interests/projects (e.g., materials, books, articles, etc.)
- You are open and willing to take the extra time finding resources to fulfill the interest of your children

Gameschooling

Gameschooling is precisely how it sounds. It uses games to intentionally educate children at home. This can be in the form of board games, card games, or even video games (Minecraft is *so* educational).

The benefit of gameschooling is that it really encourages learning through play. Consider Yahtzee, for example. As a kid, I would sit forever at the table with my Grandma honing in on my math skills without realizing it. She was always very patient with me as I counted my fingers. I still do sometimes (shhh). And the game Sorry *really* had us acquire manners.

There is so much to learn from games. Strategy, math, teamwork, turn-taking, cooperation, and decision making are just a few of the many skills you can find. There are story-based games and role-playing games, the list is endless! If you sit with the concept of gameschooling, you can see how it covers all the necessary skills and more.

A Typical Day

A typical day for a gameschooler can vary as some will use curriculum and supplement with gaming, while others will use games as the basis of their learning and use the remaining time for self-led learning.

A day of a gameschooler could look like this:
8:30 am: Breakfast
9:00 am: Games of Yahtzee and Connect 4 to warm up math skills
9:30 am: Math workbook
9:50 am: Game of Wildcraft, chatting about herbs and healing
10:20 am: Snack
10:30 am: Herb stories and coloring book
11:00 am: Tell Me a Story cards, taking turns telling made-up stories
11:30 pm: Make lunch
12:00 pm: Self-led learning for each child for the remaining of the day

Is It For You?

How to know if gameschooling is for you:
- You love playing games as a family
- You are open to using games to teach specific skills and gaining knowledge
- You want to add games to the curriculum you are using to solidify knowledge
- You are comfortable documenting their progress by journaling, taking photos, or making notes
- You have children with various learning styles
- You are open to budgeting for multiple games you'd like to add to your collection, or you are willing to create your own from online resources

Homeschooling with Unit Studies

Families who homeschool with unit studies integrate all the main subjects into one specific topic. The great part about using unit studies is that they offer a complete view of one subject rather than making each subject separate.

It makes so much sense, doesn't it? Instead of having math, art, science, and writing done in separate and completely unrelated lessons, they're worked into one topic!

Take the ocean, for example. We've studied the ocean multiple times (the first time when they were 3 and 4) because both my boys have such a great interest in it. With the ocean, we can create many art projects (art), look at habitats of various animals (science), understand depths and the pressure of the water (math), we've added shipwrecks to our ocean studies (history and social studies), and the effects of climate change on the oceans (more science). We've even planned trips to visit the ocean for the simple reason of more in-depth learning. Ways to incorporate learning into a topic are endless.

In Florida learning about shipwrecks and turtles

Using one topic to cover all subjects gives our children a much more cohesive way of learning.

A Typical Day

A typical day for young unit studies homeschoolers studying bugs could look like this:
9:00 am: Read aloud a book on ladybugs

9:20 am: Simple math, counting and recording spots on different ladybugs to determine the age

9:45 am: Practice printing the word 'ladybug' using finger-paints and then using a pencil

10:00 am: Baking ladybug-shaped cookies for snack

10:45 am: Cut and paste labeling parts of a ladybug

11:30 pm: Make lunch

12:00 pm: The life cycle of a ladybug video

12:30 pm: Hike to the woods to spot ladybugs

Is It For You?

How to know if homeschooling with unit studies is for you:

- You like the idea of choosing one topic and diving deep into that with all the other subjects (math, arts, language, science, etc.)
- You like to put pieces together to create a curriculum
- You want to choose topics of interest to your child
- You are comfortable documenting their progress by journaling, taking photos, or making notes
- You have multiple children of various ages and want everyone to learn the same topic

Literature-Based Homeschooling

Similar to using unit studies, literature-based homeschooling teaches a variety of subjects but uses a book to teach instead of a single topic.

One of our favorite books to study was Holes by Louis Sachar. We completed this book study in grade four. We not only used it to cover the basics (math, language, science, history, geography), but it also touched on social injustices, forgiveness, friendship, and fate.

The twists and turns in the plot were captivating, and the boys still talk about it to this day.

The bonus to this book (as with many great books) is that it was created into a movie. Although we all agree that the film can't ever quite capture the essence of a book, they are still fun to watch and compare at the end of a literature-based study.

Cruz drinking from a fresh coconut after reading Swiss Family Robinson

A Typical Day

A typical day for literature-based homeschoolers could look like this:
8:30 am: Snuggle up and read a chapter of the book
9:00 am: Discussion about the chapter
9:15 am: Complete spelling words and definitions of new vocabulary

9:45 am: Write about character development
10:15 am: Snack
10:30 am: Write a poem based on the recent chapter
11:00 am: Act out the chapter using lego mini-figures
11:30 am: Lunch
12:30 pm: Create a piece of art with a favorite quote from the book
1:00 pm: Draw a map of the setting from the chapter

Is It For You?

How to know if literature-based homeschooling is for you:
- You and your children love reading
- You like to put pieces together to create a curriculum (although you can also purchase full literature-based curriculums)
- You want to choose books that interest your family
- You have multiple children close in age and would enjoy learning from the same book with various levels

Waldorf Homeschooling

We blended this style with Montessori when the boys were small. Although I was once told by a Waldorf teacher that it's not possible to do both because they are opposing philosophies, I did it anyway because... Homeschool By Design.

My favorite piece of the Waldorf philosophy was its belief in storytelling. I LOVE storytelling (hence this book, know what I mean?). I also loved their nature-based themes. Stories are wrapped around nature, and the rhythm of Waldorf focuses on seasons.

The philosophy does not believe in academics until about grade 1-2 and no textbooks until grade 6. Handwork is very much encouraged, and you can often find Waldorf homeschoolers learning everything from knitting to sewing, leading to a sense of pride.

The belief of 'breathing in' and 'breathing out' activities throughout the day is a part of the Waldorf rhythm, and you'll see what I mean when you look at a typical day. 'Breathing in' activities focus inward, whereas 'breathing out' activities are more energy-producing.

A Typical Day

A typical day for a Waldorf family of homeschoolers could look like this:
9:00 am: Morning circle time, including movement (breathing out)
9:45 am: Snack preparations, everyone helps mindfully (breathing in)
10:00 am: Preparing the table and eating together (breathing out)
10:45 am: Free play (breathing in)
11:30 am: Walk in nature (breathing out)
12:15 pm: Lunch, prepared with children (breathing in)
1:00 pm: Stories or plays (breathing out)
1:45 pm: Rest and relaxation (breathing in)
2:30 pm: Crafting (breathing out)

Is It For You?

How to know if the Waldorf method of homeschooling is for you:
* You want a consistent rhythm
* You want a more natural-based approach to learning
* You want a slower pace and technique for home learning

- You want your children to have an active role in their education

Montessori Homeschooling

I wanted to be a Montessori teacher when the boys were babies. So much so I dedicated Cruz's entire first year to Montessori philosophies. I was even featured on the North American Montessori Association's website for the Montessori bedroom we designed for Cruz.

What drew me into this philosophy was using the five senses to unlock knowledge. Each child chooses their own 'work' based on what is laid out in the learning space.

Maria Montessori, Italy's first female doctor, created this approach in the early 1900s, wanting to protect the intrinsic motivation of humans and encouraging children to choose work that piques their interest. She sounds awesome.

Some important points about Montessori education are:
- Montessori-specific materials are used and are mostly natural-made
- Children are invited to participate in 'adult' work, such as cooking or cleaning, all with their own real tools (e.g., no plastic toys, but real brooms and dustpans, just child size)
- All educational materials are on low shelves for easy access by children
- The children are viewed as 'little adults' in terms of being given a lot of independence in preparing food, eating (e.g., from glass cups), etc.

I always said that if we had to send our kids to school for some reason, they'd go to a Montessori school. But how does it look at home?

A Typical Day

A typical day for young Montessori homeschoolers could look like this:

9:00 am: Children assist in preparing breakfast and setting the table (even the youngest)
9:30 am: Children clean up and assist with dishes and other chores
10:00 am: Openwork time, chosen by the children from the shelves
10:30 am: Snack and outdoor time
11:30 am: Gather together for a book
12:00 pm: Preparing lunch together, practicing manners, cleaning up
12:45 pm: Craft time
1:30 pm: Baking
2:15 pm: Outdoor time

Is It For You?

How to know if the Montessori method of homeschooling is for you:
* You are familiar with the Montessori method and believe strongly in the approach
* You have a child who is a very hand-on and tactile learner
* You are open to allow your children to take their time and learn the materials when they are ready
* You want to create an individualized curriculum based on Montessori materials

Roadschooling and Worldschooling

We travel – a lot. And not just for work (in fact, we built our work around traveling so we could travel more....life by design!), but we travel so we can learn things.

We visit Las Vegas for a month every year. The first year we did this, you know what we studied? Rocks. You know where the best place in the world to study rocks might be? The Grand Canyon – a day trip from Las Vegas. You cannot get any better than speaking to a geologist as they point to the various sections of rock when you're *at* the Grand Canyon!

Seeing the Grand Canyon for the first time

Better yet, all the national parks in the US have what's called the Junior Ranger program. This program is designed for various ages, and they complete activities before being able to be 'sworn in' by a ranger and earning their badge.

When we visited the Grand Canyon, the boys were given the workbooks to complete throughout the visit. They not only got to see the Grand Canyon, but they touched things, explored the park grounds, talked to a geologist, learned about animal habitats and ancient indigenous peoples, and completed their workbooks to earn their badge. They were so proud!

This is road schooling at its best. Learning on the road. One of my favorite parts about roadschooling is that you don't ever quite know when you will stumble upon a place of great interest. Another example using this road trip we take each year from Canada to Las Vegas – we were driving through Arizona when we kept seeing signs about a meteor crater. Having no idea what this thing was (like some tiny hold the size of a car, maybe?), we decided it was worth finding out. Well, did we ever get our socks blown off! This place was MASSIVE! It's an entire mile wide and 500 feet deep! I had zero plans to teach anything space-related during this trip, but this visit led to so many questions and deep-diving right into anything we could learn about space!

I could go on and on about the things we've learned going across our beautiful continent – visiting half the Canadian provinces and visiting close to 30 states in the US, plus various Caribbean islands. This world is so small, but you don't quite realize it until you get out there!

Worldschooling is a similar concept, except many world schooling families travel the world to immerse themselves in various cultures, rather than sticking to their continent or country. We traveled through Italy for 3 weeks and took in so much of the culture and ancient history! It's still a trip the boys speak about to this day.

We were attending the wedding of my brother-in-law but tagged on a couple of extra weeks so we could use the time to study Ancient Rome and Pompeii. Although it was quite an expensive trip, it was priceless in terms of the memories and experiences we had as a family, from touring ancient catacombs to learning

The boys admiring Mount Vesuvius from Pompeii ruins

about the gladiators at the Colosseum to standing in the massive ruins of the wealthy village of Pompeii, staring in awe at Mount Vesuvius. These are memories and moments of learning that light me up and make me want to get back out on the road and do it all over again!

A Typical Day

A typical day for a roadschooling family can look like anything. Some families travel full time and live in an RV, learning from a simple curriculum. Others take to the road for part of the year and live in a home base the rest. Since there's really no typical day (and it could look like any of the previously mentioned methods while on the road), I will leave it at that! Roadschoolers and worldschoolers learn through travel, and it always looks different.

Is It For You?

How to know if a Roadschooling or Worldschooling
method is for you:
* You love to travel
* Your choice of work allows for travel
* You want your children to be immersed in culture
  beyond their country
* You believe the world is our classroom
* You love to document learning through experiences

Project-Based Homeschooling

In project-based homeschooling, we are men-
tors to our children, providing them with resources,
supplies, and experiences they need to dig deeper into
learning of their choice (not ours...sounds a bit like unschooling, right?).

Our children's work is important! To them, it's
everything. They come to us excited about a pattern
they found on a rock and want to know exactly what it
means. They'll talk during every meal about the latest
thing in Minecraft or Peppa Pig. It's your job to take
part in the conversations. Enthusiastically ask them
questions. Celebrate their work. Share with others in
the family over dinner, brag about them over the phone
to your friends (when kids can hear).

Project-based homeschooling doesn't necessarily mean you need to throw all other curricula out the
window (I mean, you could). It means you give your
children ample free time to work on projects that mean
something to them, allowing them to fall into learning
naturally.

We like to have a list of options for the kids to refer to when they want to dig deeper into a topic. Our homeschool space has all the materials the boys would need to make any of the listed choices, and the learning they choose is entirely up to them.

This includes:
- building a model from lego or modeling clay
- creating a movie about the topic
- making a list
- writing directions
- writing a recipe
- creating a story
- painting a picture
- making a list of questions to answer
- gathering artifacts
- brainstorm
- singing a song
- inventing a game
- finding a book on the topic
- asking an expert
- collecting photos online or in old magazines
- making a bulletin board of information
- writing down important facts
- observing and documenting
- sketching
- measuring

The list goes on and on, but you get the idea!

A Typical Day

Much like unschoolers and road/worldschoolers, there isn't a particular typical day for project-based homeschoolers. Some choose to have set routines in place while others will go along with the natural flow of the day ("Mom, can we go to the dollar store so I can get popsicle sticks for my projects?"). Here's an example of one of our project-based homeschooling days from a few years back.

We once read a book about Thomas Edison (you know, the guy who invented a million things, from the incandescent lightbulb to the motion picture camera, and was also homeschooled by his mother because the school found him too disruptive). This book focused mainly on his childhood and a story about a laboratory he had as a kid.

Avery, being quite the inventor himself, was in awe of this idea. A lab at home! It's just what he wanted. He collected materials from around the house – from baking soda to food coloring – to build his own lab.

Avery building his lab

We visited the dollar store that same day to purchase small jars for his collection of materials. Avery labeled each carefully and lined them up. He pulled out science goggles to protect himself and found an old magnifying glass to get a closer look at his collection.

Avery mixed different items together to see what would happen. I would take notes for him, and he would create recipes of his various experiments, noting what happened (mostly nothing). This led to a high interest in science for the next couple of weeks.

Is It For You?

How to know if project-based homeschooling is for you:
- You believe children learn best by following their passions or interests
- You are comfortable documenting their progress by journaling, taking photos, or making notes
- You have children with various learning styles
- You are comfortable being more of a mentor role in providing your children with resources they need for their different interests/projects (e.g., materials, books, articles, etc.)
- You are open and willing to take the extra time finding resources to fulfill the interest of your children

Eclectic Homeschooling

When you see pieces of various styles that you want to include in your homeschool, this is eclectic homeschooling. And, really, Homeschool By Design! You're taking what you love and making it all yours. Although we tend to be on the side of unschooling, I suppose we are more relaxed homeschoolers as I like to cover math and writing as a part of our daily routine. We do toss in a unit study here or there (hello, Harry Potter!), and we definitely road school for about 1/4 of the year. I use a lot of the rhythmic ideas of Waldorf education, and project-based homeschooling is our jam.

Wait...maybe we really are eclectic!

This didn't happen overnight, and it likely won't for you, either. You may try a few different methods before realizing that you want to piece different methods together.

A Typical Day

What if I just share what our general schedule looks like? When we aren't traveling, this is what we typically do. I've thrown in the times, but these fluctuate, as we aren't set to a specific time table. Of course, we throw in field trips, visits to the library or thrift store for some cool books, but generally, this is what it looks like:

7:00 am: Boys wake up and watch a couple of YouTube videos on how to be a better gamer

7:30 am: Head to the gaming room and play some Fortnite with friends from around the world (Europe, all over the USA, other areas of Canada)

9:00 am: Exercise on the mini-trampoline

9:15 am: Make their own breakfasts, and sometimes mine!

9:30 am: Complete online math and writing games

10:30 am: Study what they are interested in – at the time of this writing, it's body systems...you know, poop and stuff

11:30 Snuggle up on the couch where I read our recent chapter book to them

12:00 pm: Lunch, made as a family or by the boys

12:30 pm: 20-minute walk with the dog

1:00 pm: Self-led time – Cruz leans towards coding, designing, creating VR worlds while Avery creates things, invents things, or takes things apart and puts them back together

3:00 pm: Friends come over to play

Is It For You?

How to know if eclectic homeschooling is for you:
- You like various parts of different styles
- You have tried different methods and want to blend them
- You are open to finding different pieces of curriculum or making it up as you go
- You are comfortable documenting their progress by journaling, taking photos, or making notes
- You feel like more than one method of homeschooling is for you

Whew, that's a LOT of different styles of homeschooling – and new definitions are popping up all the time!

One important thing to remember is that every single style has within it a sliding scale of strict to loosely-based families. No homeschoolers are the same. The examples given of a typical day could still look nothing like a typical day for some. So to any veteran homeschoolers reading this, no sending me messages in all caps telling me how wrong the day of an unschooler looks (I've been one myself!). Deal? Sweet.

Finding Curriculum

Oh, the options! Depending on the type of person you are, this could be really fun or really intimidating. For me, it's so joyous, like my birthday! I love opening a box of fresh, new curriculum! It is filled with so much inspiration and knowledge, and I imagine it filling my children's heads with so much goodness.

If finding a curriculum is less enthusiastic for you, then I suggest starting off slow. Join the Homeschool By Design group on Facebook or another group based on your style of homeschooling. Then search the group for curriculum suggestions. You'll find so much. It's a great place to start with minimal intimidation and maximum support.

There are various types of curriculum to choose from. Sometimes it feels like there are as many curriculums out there as there are children...a lot, right?

So how do you choose which one is right for you? There are a few things to consider:

1. How your children learn.
2. Whether you want an online curriculum or actual in-your-hand curriculum or both.
3. If you're looking for an all-in-one curriculum with every subject laid out or if you'd rather piece curriculum together or whether you want curriculum at all!
4. If you're going to include the specific morals and values you may have in your family.
5. The reviews on any curriculum you're considering.
6. Whether you are required to use something specific based on the laws where you live.
7. If you want your curriculum to include assessments or not.

Options for curriculum include in-your-hand curriculum that you order online and arrive at your doorstep to actual online options where the work is done exclusively from a computer or tablet.

When it comes to traditional homeschooling curriculum, the information is laid out for you. There are activities you follow in a specific order, and they often include some sort of test or assessment or learning. Your children complete their own grade levels and follow closely to what their friends are learning in traditional schools.

Montessori and Waldorf curriculums will often have laid out lesson plans as well.

If you look at a curriculum for a specific topic for a unit study, let's say a unit on bugs, they are often created by other homeschoolers. They may not necessarily include a specific schedule of when to teach it. It's up to you as the parent to decide when and how much to teach. You also want to document their learning if there are no assessments with the unit.

As a project-based homeschooler or an unschooler, there's no curriculum wrapped around this (but lots of books for you to read). As the parent, you'll want to set up a system for documenting the learning taking place (especially if required by law).

Whatever you use as curriculum, secularhome-schooler.com has an incredible resource with hundreds of curriculum options, the subjects they cover, and links to their websites all in an easy-to-navigate list.

If you were feeling stressed about the 'documenting the learning' part, I kept bringing up, don't stress! Next, we're headed to **Mechanism Island**, where we will learn how to plan our days and be pro documenters.

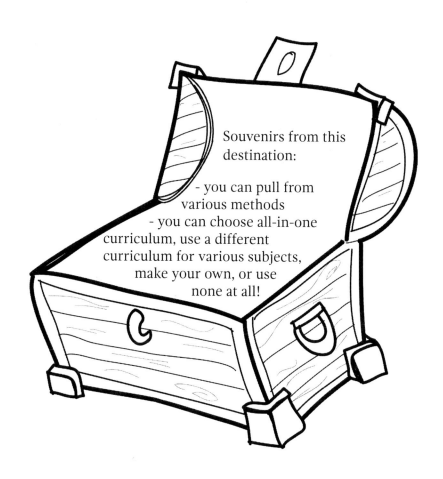

Souvenirs from this destination:

- you can pull from various methods
- you can choose all-in-one curriculum, use a different curriculum for various subjects, make your own, or use none at all!

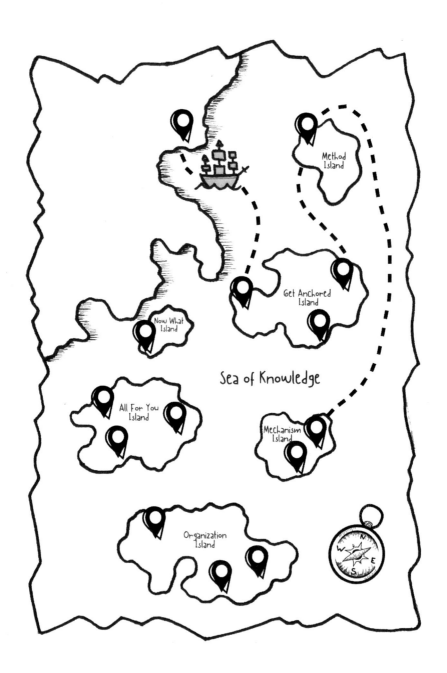

All the ways to plan your days

WE'VE ARRIVED AT **Mechanism Island**! It is here where we will explore the mechanics behind homeschooling – the planning and the documenting. Once you leave here, you'll have an idea of what your homeschool days will look like, plus plans in place to document all the learning.

Let's jump into the destination of planning. Whether you call it a schedule, a routine, a rhythm, or a flow, we all have a structure for our day. We have a general time we eat, play, visit friends, go on adventures, and learn.

Should you set up a schedule?

This is a question I get a lot. Like, a *lot*. It's even something I covered recently in a TV interview about homeschooling.

"What does your schedule look like?"

Well, my friends, I can't say we really have one.

We have more of a rhythm to our day than a set schedule. It wasn't always this way – I kept a pretty strict routine for those early years of homeschooling.

Back then, I needed a schedule, so I felt like I was teaching the learning I wanted them to cover. The boys needed a schedule because they were the kind of young kids who needed something in place. It made their world feel safe when they had a schedule. Without one, they felt out of control because they didn't know what was happening next.

Today, a strict schedule, like the ones we had for years, would no longer make us feel calm. Instead, it makes us feel restricted. We made this change about two years ago when my boys couldn't really dig deep into a subject they loved because it would be time to move on to something else. That's when I knew it was time to move to a rhythm versus a schedule. Home-school By Design, right?

If you ask me, "Should I set up a schedule," my answer is, "Only you will know."

Some things to ask yourself about a schedule are:
* Will it bring a sense of calm to my children and me?
* Will it help me to feel organized in teaching them?
* Do I want to make a schedule because other people are making schedules or because I believe it would work best for my children or myself?
* Do I want a strict schedule or and open schedule? A schedule or a rhythm to our day? Go with the flow or stick to a routine?
* How many different ages am I planning for?

If you know you need a set schedule, don't feel like it has to follow the traditional school schedule (although it can if it works for you). Your schedule can look how you want it to look.

Perhaps you want to cover all the 'traditional' subjects with worksheets and workbooks. Your schedule might look like each subject taught each day.

Or maybe you want to use YouTube videos, TV shows, movies, or documentaries as a base for learning. Your schedule might look like show-watching in the morning with breakfast, followed by some planned activities to go with it. Hands-on stuff for the rest of the day – maybe the kids want to bake after watching a baking show, or perhaps they want to go outside and look for bugs after watching National Geographic.

Or maybe you're a family with kids who learn best when things are hands-on. Your schedule might be more involved in experiments, arts and crafts, music, and movement.

Or maybe you work night shifts and sleep during the day, so most of the homeschooling takes place in the evenings before you go to work and on weekends.

All of these things should be considered when planning a schedule. A few other things to consider are:

- What time will my children be ready to learn?
- Do my children learn best while sitting, moving, doing activities?
- Do my children require lots of breaks?
- Do I want a strict schedule to follow or a loose outline of things to cover each day?

How to set up your day

The way you set up your day is focused mostly on how your children work best, what time they work best, and the style of homeschool you choose.

For example, if you are a traditional home-schooler, you may have everything set to a schedule, and you set up your day that way. You may start your morning routine with an agenda or a calendar - looking at the day while singing songs about the days of the week. If you have older children, maybe you spend mornings writing out affirmations and doing yoga. Perhaps you do some gratitude journaling or some light yoga. Your day could then move into a flow with various subjects and breaks throughout the morning and into the afternoon with the finishing day of around three or four o'clock like traditional school.

Other homeschoolers may choose more of a rhythm of their day. Rhythms are an essential part of the Waldorf philosophy. They are used to encourage a feeling of security, especially for younger children who find comfort in regular and expected things. This kind of day may look like listening quietly to a story and being peaceful. Then the children move outside for running and playing in the backyard. Then they come back in for a quiet craft and then going to the park for some active play. This rhythm of in and out, in and out, is repeated during the day. It's not necessarily attached to a specific time.

Then there are unschoolers – the free-spirited of the homeschooling world. Every day can look different, every day is living life and learning from it.

The following example of our days is exactly that: *our* days. It's like me sharing what we had for dinner; it'll be different from most everyone else's dinners. My hope in sharing is so you can see we designed our homeschool as we needed to; we adjusted as we went along. We changed it and shifted when the needs of our boys changed and shifted. It's by no means an example of anyone else but me!

Examples of Our Days

Babies to Toddlers

Although Montessori and Waldorf's philosophies are on opposite ends, we used both when the boys were small. I'm talking birth to around four or five. I had shelves, a part of the Montessori philosophy,

Our Montessori shelves when they were an infant & toddler

and these shelves would be filled with baskets and simple wooden toys, which covered both the Montessori and the Waldorf philosophies. In the mornings we would sing songs and read a book. I had made a felt board out of felt and cardboard, and we would use felt characters on the board as I shared a story. I'd even make them myself, printing characters on cardstock and gluing felt to the back.

A favorite book of mine – and I'm sure of theirs – was The Very Hungry Caterpillar. We must have read that book a thousand times. Actually. We had a mini-board book version as well as a gigantic board book meant for a teacher in a classroom. I found it at a garage sale for next to nothing. #homeschoolingonabudget

We would usually start our day with one of these books. I would sit on the floor with them as they would search around the different shelves picking things to work with (their play is their work). I remember having this long mirror sitting vertically on the floor. When Cruz was still a baby and not even able to sit up, he would lie on his tummy, trying to look up at a mirror. He could do this forever.

During this time, Avery and I would work on an activity for his level. He might take a cloth and a spray bottle and spend 15 or 20 minutes scrubbing the windows, or he would take the blocks and organize them based on size and color.

They would both be helpful during the preparation of food as, according to Montessori philosophy, children are like little adults. They both had their own small, dull knives at about one year old. Although they could only cut things like bread, it gave them the technique to understand what it meant to cut. It also gave them the feeling of responsibility that came with participating in preparing the food for each meal. I remember taking out spices that I would use and letting Avery sniff them. Every time he would smell them, he would say "Mmmmm' even if it wasn't that great. So sweet!

These days were slow, present, and mindful. Well, for the most part. We always remember the good, not the 5 am wake-ups and non-napping days where we thought we might never make it out of baby-hood alive.

Preschoolers

As their age and abilities increased, our days looked a little bit different. We would take slow walks around the block to observe the small details around us. On rainy days we might look for worms, damp mornings for snails, and every day for birds. We would use the seasons to compare the trees in our neighborhood.

A lot of our talk would involve counting or naming colors as we would go on walks or bake cookies or even walk down to the basement.

How many steps are we taking?
How many trees do you see?
How many worms are there?

Everything could be related back to the skills they needed to know at that stage. But the essential part of these early years had always been play. So much research available shows how vital this age is for play. Children learn through play. Even things that don't seem like play to us is play to them, like cleaning.

Do you ever notice how badly toddlers want to clean, but with elementary children, they hate chores? It's no longer play for them; now it's work.

Under the age of 4, 30 minutes of direct 'learning' is all that you should consider (and some methods even believe that's too much). The majority of their time is spent with imaginative play and exploring the world. It's all they need! They learn about the world around them by playing house or doctor and cleaning or building with child-sized tools. They mimic the world around them as a way to understand it. At this stage, we focused a lot of their 'work' around this concept.

***

A couple of years ago, I ended up with an infection from a cut in my finger, which led to swelling and IV drop of antibiotics for a few days, then eventually lancing and draining the finger. I bet you're squirming right now, but let me tell you how awesome this was to my boys!

I was a hero. After the lancing and draining, I had to shove soaked gauze into the wound to pack it each morning, then remove it and do it again at night. They thought this was both the coolest thing ever and the grossest thing ever.

Our entire learning during that week revolved around my finger. There was a possibility I needed stitches, so my boys found our dog's toys around the house with holes in them and practiced sewing. Many toys required fixing.

They put masks on, just like in a real doctor's office, and taught themselves different stitches. They fixed all of the dog's toys with various stitching types. They also watched a few doctor series on TV to get the gist of what it meant to be a doctor.

They came with me to my appointments to see the hospital in action, and all their play that week had something to do with injuries, hospitals, or doctor visits. It was awesome and just goes to show that learning can be influenced in many ways.

Sewing up the dog's toys

Also, kids use play to work out their emotions. As much as Mom might be tearing up from the pain of the gauze, they might need to process that emotion for themselves. Play is the best way to do that. It allows them to process and move on.

Although this story took place when they were in the early elementary age, it just goes to show how kids of all ages require play to learn and work through heavy feelings.

***

Early Elementary Age – ages 5-8

When the boys were at a school age, we had more of a structured routine in place. I added set chores for each boy. I purchased a curriculum we used, and we would sit down every day at the same time and complete our work throughout the day and into the afternoon. We would take breaks for lunch and to also play outside with our neighbors who are also homeschooling.

This worked for us for a couple of years, but in my heart, I always felt like it wasn't what I wanted my homeschool to look like. Comparison is the thief of joy. I was always comparing myself to my fellow homeschoolers and felt I had to do it the way they did, or I would be 'doing it wrong.' More on this later.

I also didn't believe I was doing a good enough job if I didn't have set times in place. I would get nervous if I took my kids to the park or the library or the grocery store in fear of other people judging why my children weren't in school. And if someone asked why they weren't in school and I had to tell them we were homeschoolers, I always felt guilty that we were out during the time they were supposed to be in school.

It took me years to finally come into my own place and learn that what was best for my children was what I always felt in my heart, and that was closer to an unschooling experience. This brings us to our middle elementary age.

Middle Elementary Age – ages 9-11

It was somewhere between grades 3 and 4, where I finally stepped into my own power as a homeschooling mom. I stopped caring about what others would post; I stopped comparing and thinking I wasn't doing enough. I stopped trying to prove myself to family members, even though no one was ever questioning me.

Over this time Avery turned 10. I remember reading something somewhere that said it takes 10 years to be an expert at something. Avery turning 10 meant I had been homeschooling for 10 years (oh yes, I did all sorts of homeschooling-type things with him when he was a baby).

I was an expert.

That was the time I shifted without even knowing it. I trusted in myself and saw these little humans as little men. Their personalities wove themselves into our lives as adults, asking adult-like questions and pondering over world problems right alongside us. These children weren't children anymore.

With these changes of personality came changes in the way we homeschooled. Parenting became less 'telling them what to do' and more 'including them in the choices of what to do.'

Unschooling also appeared in our lives. We moved with the topics the boys wanted to learn about. A lot of technology-driven ideas, that's for sure! A question about Instagram filters turned into Cruz learning how to create Instagram filters for one of Daddy's festival clients. He was only eight. But that's the thing: when children are allowed to lead themselves in their learning and we, as parents, provide those resources and opportunities, our children have the best outcomes. They were allowed to choose.

I look at it this way: if we have the option to choose our career path, what's holding us back from allowing our children to choose their topics for learning?

My own personal experience ends here, as my boys are still in this age group. To look at typical plans for older children, ask Google or search on Pinterest for bloggers who share their points of view.

Our Current Schedule

Although I posted a quick synopsis in our last destination, I will go into more detail to give you an example of how our days are loosely planned. I call our schedule a 'rhythm,' and it changes as we do. No times are set in stone, and it often changes as we have various activities we participate in. Currently, this is what our days look like.

Around 7-8 am: The boys wake up on their own and join their friends in Fortnite. This is their social time with their friends from around the world. How have they made these friends? Through online classes. So awesome!

Around 9 am: We come together in the kitchen to make breakfast. The boys make their own breakfast and sometimes offer to make mine (bonus!). We take all our vitamins and supplements, talk about how they did in Fortnite, discuss anything current in the world, chat about what we want the day to look like.

Around 9:30 am: They begin their 'homeschool' day. I create a list each morning in a Note on my phone (which connects to their iPads) for items to be completed. This is based on their recent interests. For example, they are currently interested in herbs. On the list, I'll have a link to a video for them to watch on the herb of the day, some research to do, a coloring/labeling page, words to define, art ideas, and any other resource I can provide them within this topic. We also include articles to read/answer questions about, some snuggling time on the couch and reading and anything else that might pertain to a specific day (e.g., we have special chats during certain moon phases). They also have memberships to math and writing game sites. They play these daily. This style leans closer to eclectic homeschooling, as we blend various methods (including unschooling in our afternoons).

Around 12 am: We have lunch together, clean up, then the boys can choose to dig deeper into the learning from the morning or find another activity/interest to work on. Sometimes it's producing music, sometimes it's building structures with Lego, sometimes it's learning how to design a logo, sometimes it's working on coding, sometimes it's exploring the backyard for bugs. This is different every.single.day. It's my job to document what they are learning as they follow their passions (stay tuned, you'll love the documenting destination).

At 3 am: The boys play with their friends, home from traditional school.

Around 5 pm: Dinner is ready, and we eat, chat about Fortnite (it never gets old in this house), go over our day, and learn anything else.

Around 5:30 pm: We take our dog for a family walk.

Around 6 pm: We have a family game of Fortnite. Yes. My husband and I are addicts, too, and I currently teach Fortnite classes on Outschool.com.

Around 6:30 pm: The boys are free for the evening to make choices on their own. Sometimes they want to watch something on TV, sometimes they want to play board games, but most of the time it's the choice to play with friends again.

Around 8 pm: We spend the last hour before bed doing chores. They put away all the day's dishes in the dishwasher, do laundry that needs to be put away, etc. This is also their fav time to read or write books. I can't for the *life* of me to get them to do these things during the day, and I've come to accept that. I suppose there's something magical about the sun going down and snuggling in bed with a journal and fancy pens or a book to read.

Around 9:30 pm: Avery is asleep, and Cruz stays up reading for another hour. He is his father.

So that's our family rhythm! We very loosely move through our day, and I never know where one particular day might take us. When the first human space launch happened with a commercial rocket, we spent a couple of weeks focused on space. All other topics went out of the window because they wanted to eat up as much as they could about space travel. This works for us.

I hope my rhythm has been helpful to those looking to schedule...or not! Remember that words matter and use words that fit your family: schedule, routine, or rhythm.

Take the time to learn what works best for your family without comparing it to me or anyone else. Do you feel the freedom in that? Only you know what your family's days should look like to create the most peace and enjoyment.

Planning The Bigger Picture

Scheduling Yearly

The yearly plan is a big, important one, but still something you can update and revise as the year moves on. I used to get really hung up on myself for this one. If I planned to complete a particular curriculum and didn't get it done in the allotted time I set for us, I believed I had failed my children. *That's it! No one will succeed in this house because Mom didn't get through Canada's entire history!*

Ah, how I appreciate that naive version of myself. I don't even recognize that girl anymore. Thank goodness. I've come around to realize that not everything will get done, and that's okay. But that's where I was stuck in my yearly plan. If I wrote it down, it had to get done. I'm here to tell you, type-A personalities, it doesn't have to be that way.

Scheduling yearly is helpful because you get a bigger picture than just a monthly or weekly schedule. But if your daughter's cheer team makes it to the finals and you have to travel for 2 weeks, throw curriculum out the window! I'm giving you permission! The life lessons she will learn during her two weeks will far outweigh that review on decimals.

Use a yearly schedule as more of a wish list. It's the plan that gives a gentle overview of how you wish your year to go. As it moves along, check-in every quarter to see what needs to be added, adjusted, or downright taken away.

Use it to mark down the various curriculums you are using, if any, or mark current interests.

Scheduling Monthly

Monthly plans can bring all the pieces together. Here we include any appointments, special occasions, and the plans for them (we always take time off for each person's birthday), activities, and field trips. You have a general idea of what your children will cover and a few goals for their learning.

You can also plan the month backward with what's been learned – I love doing this! As unschoolers or project-based/child-led learners, backward planning is the place to be. With each week and month that goes on, you document in your planner all the interests and projects of your children. You can then add in the general learning topics covered *after* the months have gone by.

For example, in September, you visited an apple farm. From there, your children wanted to dive into all things apples – from baking to classifying and learning the life cycle of an apple. When you backward plan in October, you will note that September covered all things apples. Fun, right? So instead of planning the curriculum for September, you document what's been learned and then add it to the plan after. I love this! It relieves all the pressure and allows for all the deep learning without a timed agenda.

Scheduling Weekly

Some people like to have a list of things to complete within the week. Here, the list of activities may get finished before the week is done. Sometimes items don't get completed and need to be added onto the following week.

Weekly schedules help you get an overview of what's coming up. By knowing days for playdates or other scheduled activities, you can gauge how your learning time will fit in.

Scheduling Daily

For those who want to keep a stricter schedule, it could look like traditional school where lessons are covered one after another. Sometimes it looks like a timed schedule (e.g., math at 9 am, and history at 9:45 am), or maybe it moves along as your child takes the time they need to do the work. There might be days where the math takes much longer than usual, and maybe you skip over spelling that day because he needed more time to grasp the subject of math.

For others, a planned out day might not go any further than the time they eat breakfast – they move with the flow of interests, errands, and activities preplanned. Then there is everything else between, as you noticed when we covered the plethora of homeschooling methods.

Homeschooling allows the learning to take place as it needs to for full understanding. Let them take advantage of this time at home to really dig into concepts as they need to. Your daily schedule, rhythm, or flow will reflect this.

A Few Notes on Planning Your Days

As I've mentioned, how you plan your day (or not) will vary from family to family, but I want to say a few essential things:

1. Teachers deal with 25+ kids in a classroom. There's lots of time taken to discipline, time for kids to complete work or busywork, time for them to get in line and wait for the bell, time for recess and lunch. The actual instruction time varies between about 45 minutes to around 1.5 hours a day, depending on the grade. So remember that when you feel pressure to keep your kids educated all day long! For us, homeschoolers, our actual 'schoolwork' (which looks different for every family), takes place in about 2 hours. Be okay with that! Let go of the guilt that you need to have them at a desk with work-sheets from 9-3.

2. Life is 'school work.' Every single thing you do at home is teaching them a skill. In fact, we recently made mason jar soup mixes. Math, science, reading, and geography can all be touched on here (measurements, why water softens beans, following a recipe, and where ingredients are found in the world). Life equals learning.

3. If you are a person who thrives in routine or with a schedule (and so do your kids), check out Pinterest for great ideas about scheduling for different grades. You can also create a rough plan in your Field Guide.

4. Leave plenty of space for boredom. We've been taught to believe that children's schedules need to be packed, so they aren't bored. According to these false beliefs, boredom leaves too much space for

terrible behavior. Well, it doesn't take much to realize how North American children are more anxious than ever. There is no time to be slow. Bring that gift back to your children. It's hard at first, mainly if they are used to having a strict schedule to follow. But let them be bored, let them complain. I promise you they will eventually access their imagination and come up with something to do. If not, you could always offer them chores.

Types of Planning

Loop scheduling – This schedule doesn't assign a specific subject to each day. You just list all the subjects you want to cover and use the list as your rotating schedule. Loop schedules are the best when something comes up and you need to put a pause on homeschooling. Maybe a friend is in town or there's a leak in the ceiling that needs your immediate attention. With a loop schedule, nothing gets missed. You can take the time you need for other things and come right back to the schedule.

In this example from a few years ago, you can see I had two subjects listed in our daily schedule and the others in our loop. Math and language were everyday topics. The remaining we looped through. You can even go one step further. Let's say you want to teach science and music twice each week. In the loop, you would add one more listing for science and one more for music. Then, as you rotate through the schedule, you'll cover an extra science and music for every history, art, and social studies.

Set schedule – Much like a traditional classroom setting, this schedule would include particular classes on particular days. Let's say science on Tuesday and Thursdays, while math, spelling, and grammar are daily. The schedule would be set for certain times of the day, the same every day, and would be followed in the same way week-to-week. This schedule doesn't allow for more in-depth studies but does keep core concepts consistently in the children's minds.

Block scheduling – This is similar to what you see in high school or college. The year is divided into terms, and each term covers a set of subjects. For example, one term may cover spelling, grammar, art, and history, while another term may cover geography, science, math, and reading. This allows for more in-depth knowledge and time to understand various concepts, but can also cause core concepts to be forgotten over time.

Scheduling types may vary from child to child, depending on their age. If you have a much older high school child, their schedule will differ significantly from that of an early elementary child. They will also require a lot less of your time while learning for longer hours.

It will also vary based on your particular family needs. The single working homeschooling mom to three teens will differ completely from the stay-at-home full-time homeschooling mom of four kids under ten. Teaching multiple children is a totally different schedule, and I get to that in the *Common Homeschool Questions* destination on **All For You Island**.

You also want to consider the timing of your homeschool. If you travel in the winter, perhaps you take a break during that time and homeschool through the summer.

For us, we learn all year round and don't take breaks. Our breaks are naturally inserted throughout the year when we feel we need them (e.g., when we are not feeling well or if we randomly decide to drive 20 hours to Disney...true story).

This is where you show up to design your schedule as you want. Now that you have the knowledge come up with a plan on how you want to set your days.

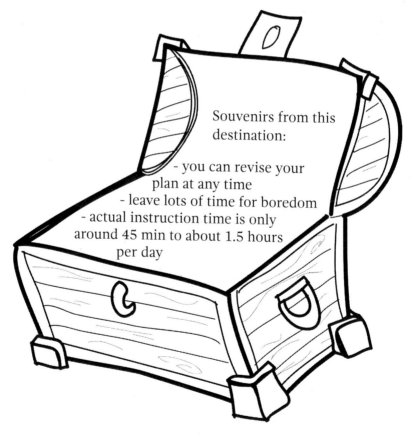

Souvenirs from this destination:

- you can revise your plan at any time
- leave lots of time for boredom
- actual instruction time is only around 45 min to about 1.5 hours per day

Simple steps to keep track of education

WELCOME TO YOUR next destination: Documenting Learning. Although it sounds a bit intimidating (like, hey there, I'm a parent, not a lawyer), documenting your children's learning is actually pretty fun. In all honesty, it's another one of my favorite parts about homeschooling!

Here's the thing: with a well-documented homeschool, you can look back on these times with great memories and see all the things you've done together. You get to see their growth over time, the extraordinary experiences, field trips, and random excursions. The fussing over a caterpillar and who will get to raise it. The winters spent baking bread and summers spent squealing through the sprinkler. Documenting is worth doing.

Designing the right kind of documenting for you is the key to your happiness. If you detest doodling and free-style planning with blank journals, bullet journaling will not be your thing. Using a planner to document is probably your way to go if you love crisp new planners and color-coding.

In designing your best version of documenting, you also have to look at the laws you need to follow.
- What are you required to document?
- Do you have to track attendance?
- Do they need report cards?
- Are there tests or exam scores you need to record?
- Are you tracking any medical needs?

There is a lot to consider when looking at requirements for documentation. Check off the ones that apply to the laws where you live and add them to your field guide.

There might be some other fun things you want to keep track of, too! Here's a list of things you may also want to add to your tracking:
- Movies/TV shows watched and a note about what was learned.
- Baking or cooking that is done together.
- Books read, questions asked about the book, other learning inspired by the book.
- Lists of questions your child has asked that you want to gather items for (e.g., "Mom, how to robins build a nest?" may lead you to find some YouTube videos on this topic, printables about robins, e-books on bird science, gather craft supplies to make a nest, etc.).
- Trackers for things like exercise (eg: daily yoga on YouTube), books read, online courses completed, virtual tours to museums, etc.

Why Document?

In my very personal opinion, the number one reason you should document your homeschool days is the same reason we record our baby's weight when they're born, the day they took their first steps, and every birthday party they've ever had.

We document because they're here on this planet.

They are important.

They have a story, and we want it captured for generations to come!

The second reason a person may document their homeschool days is, as I just mentioned because it's a part of the requirements in their country, state, province, county, etc. I choose to go with reason number one as the biggest reason I document. Know why? Because it makes it feel fun! And it sort of makes me feel like the historian in the family, keeping our stories alive. Except I don't get paid.

Where to document?

If you're anything like me, you've got stacks of half-completed journals and have bought out the stationery sets at the local dollar store more than once. Documenting is my fav.

There are so many ways you can document. There's bullet journaling, agendas, and binders, OH MY! Then there's notebooks and sticky notes and blogging and phone apps...the options are endless!

It's overwhelming to some who aren't such lovers of documenting, but I promise I'll make this fun (even if it's just a wee bit fun for you). Starting is straightforward.

Choose what you love
Gather your supplies
Start documenting

How to Document Learning

There are a variety of ways you can document your child's learning. It can be as simple as note-taking on your phone to as complicated as making pretty bullet journaling pages, depending on your style.

Remember: it's your design.

Consider your why, what's important to you, and the long-game for your homeschool.

Here are some of the ways you can document what your kids are doing:

1. Have a folder for each child and include a couple of pieces of work in it from each week. This could be worksheets (if you use them), artwork, crafting, and any photos you may have taken of bigger projects.

2. Use an agenda to make a list of things done each day. You can use an agenda to keep track in two ways: 1) to plan out what you want the kids to learn each day, or 2) to write down what the kids have done each day

3. Use a bullet journal to document questions they ask, things they've done, explorations of the backyard,

etc. I LOVE making things look pretty with stickers, washi tape, and doodles. I once went through a stage where I only used a bullet journal to keep track of the things my boys asked about, things we did together, and printed photos to track some of our more significant learning moments. Looking back on those journals is such fun!

4. A simple 'to-do' list in the notes section of your phone to keep track of daily activities needed to be done or that has been completed.

5. Use an app, like Paper (by Dropbox), to post your photos with a note about the learning taking place. You can make quick notes each time you notice 'learning' and attach a quick photo. We've also been using the Notes app for tracking each day and what they learn. I use the Notes app to make lists for our boys because they currently love checklists (even if it's for their own projects). I share the Note with their iPads, and they check off their work as they do it. Works for scheduling and for tracking – it's a win-win!

6. Create a digital or actual scrapbook to track photos and use captions to keep a note of the learning taking place. There are many digital scrapbook companies out there that will use your pictures and captions and turn them into hardcover books for you to enjoy.

7. Start a blog and post about different things you're all doing.

8. Start a private Facebook group to share what you're learning (this can just be for your own documentation, but also fun for other family members to 'watch' what your kids are doing).

9. Create a photo album using Pages or Microsoft Word to track learning with photos each week.

10. A napkin. Because, hey, maybe that's all you can find in the heat of a learning moment!

We've done all the different types of documenting over the years. I've had a full 'teacher' binder with actual schedules when it worked for us. I've also done bullet journaling filled with photos we printed with a mini printer. We've made portfolios at the end of each year with samples of their work, and have also documented everything in apps like Paper.

Just like how you teach at home, documenting can look any way you want it to look. This is a part of your Homeschool By Design.

Be honest with yourself when choosing a way to document. You may love the idea of scrapbooking, but if you're a work-at-home mama who is homeschooling four kids and is the only one in the house who will clean the cat litter, will you actually have the time to scrapbook? Maybe. But check in with yourself anyway and be sure the documentation you choose is right for you.

Also, be okay with scraping the initial idea you had. If you're 3 weeks into your perfect documentation binder but find it's impossible to keep it with you when you need it because it's so massive, maybe you start again with a different system.

How to Document Learning in Everyday Activities

It's one thing to document the easy stuff (like attendance), but what about those everyday learning moments that aren't a part of a full curriculum? What if you use unit studies, unschooling, or the kids are working on a project on their own? That's where your handy Learning Lens comes back into play.

One of my favorite things to do is to use my Learning Lens to play a game with myself that involves coming up with as many learning possibilities for a topic as possible. I know it sounds ridiculous, but hear me out.

Let's take making a salad, for example. There's so much we can learn here, and you can gauge it to the age of the child.

Reading/Writing:
- researching a recipe for salad dressing
- copying out a recipe
- creating your own salad recipe
- printing the word 'salad' or the letter 's' for the younglings

Art:
- comparing and contrasting colors of vegetables
- understanding the pigments of vegetables (also could be science-related!)
- plating the salad in a fancy way, adding sprouts to make it look nice
- watching a YouTube video on how professional chefs create beautifully-presented salads

Social Studies:
- where each vegetable comes from

- how long it takes the vegetable to go from the farm to our plate
- how each vegetable has been used historically
- how different cultures may use the vegetables differently

Math:
- counting vegetable pieces as they go into the bowl
- learning fractions when cutting up a tomato into quarters
- measuring ingredients for the dressing
- categorizing the vegetables based on shape, color, size

Science:
- nutrients in vegetables and how they benefit the body
- how a salad spinner works to pull out the water from the lettuce
- how the plants grow (vine, underground, etc.)

How fun was that?! I promise it gets easier with practice. The more you view the world from your Learning Lens, the easier this becomes!

Let's try another one. These are actually from my personal documenting from a year ago when my boys were playing Fortnite.

History
- timeline of every season
- character development over the seasons
- Aztecs, Vikings, Asia, pirates, Medieval period (these were all areas on the map in the past)
- how the game developed over time

Music & Art
- creating gaming music on Garage Band

- comparing how music feels when we play vs. no music when we play
- learning the emotes (dances in Fortnite)
- creating Fortnite cosutumes

At ComicCon with our homemade Fortnite costumes

Math
- game stats (fortnitetracker.com)
- accuracy percentage
- comparing team eliminations
- leaderboard statistics
- health and shield percentages and fractions
- V-bucks and exchanging real money into V-bucks
- spending money on skins, managing money, budgeting

Science
- physics: how fast you can drop from the bus vs. how far you want to land on the map and whether you should use the glider vs. free drop
- compare food we eat as humans for supporting our bodies to shield potion for characters in Fortnite to keep their health
- learning which materials are best for building
- learning different building structures and how their strength can hold up in a battle

Literature
- reading Fortnite guidebooks
- learning how to search for Fortnite books at the library or on Amazon

Strategy Skills
- coming up with battle plans, what works and what doesn't
- utilizing different weapons for different purposes

Film
- Fortnite documentary on Amazon Prime
- YouTube skills videos
- Creating their own Fortnite videos (lighting, voice-over, editing, etc.)

Planning
- Fortnite party planning with themed foods
- planning activities related to Fortnite

It's so fun to find notes like these! It reminds me of the benefits of their passion.

To this list, I would add some of the current stuff my kiddos have been working on in Fortnite:

- developing an online course for other kids on learning how to play
- designing Fortnite skins
- creating a custom map
- designing games and inviting their friends to play
- studying map skills, landforms, and bodies of water using Fortnite
- launching their own clan, including tryouts, and designing a logo and certificate for anyone that makes it in

Many of these ideas can be applied to various other video games as well. So if you wonder if your children are learning anything from Mario 3D, Minecraft, or Roblox, yes, yes, they are.

Now it's your turn! Think about an activity your children participated in over the last 24 hours and see how many various topics they covered. Refer to your Field Guide if you'd like to mark it all down (look at you, already documenting!).

Say buh-bye to **Mechanism Island** because **Organization Island** is our next port.

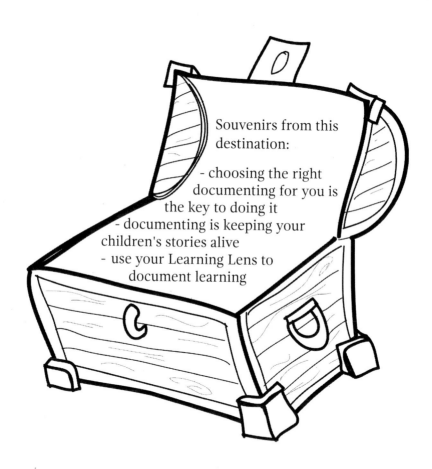

Souvenirs from this destination:

- choosing the right documenting for you is the key to doing it
- documenting is keeping your children's stories alive
- use your Learning Lens to document learning

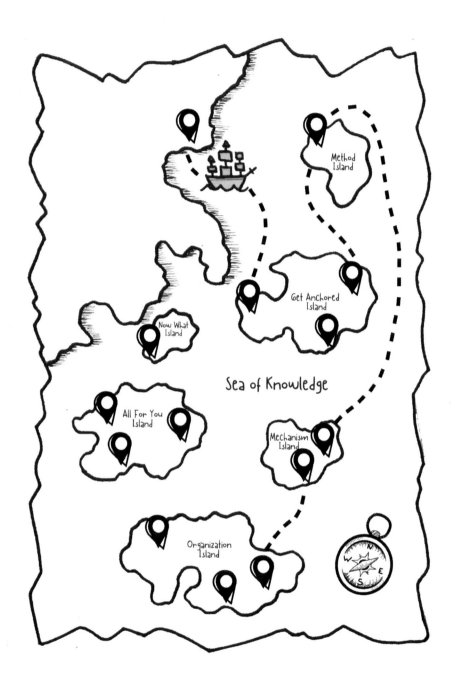

Plan for the place

HERE WE ARE! **Organization Island** – which is just what you need at this point. We've anchored ourselves and learned about all the methods and mechanisms to homeschooling, so now it's time to organize it all. Take a moment to breathe it in – you've come such a long way!

Our first destination is *Organizing Your Space.* There's just something about a freshly organized space that makes you never want your kids to touch it, right? Unfortunately, they must. You know, to learn and all.

Organizing your space is what will set the tone for learning. An inviting area with pillows and a comfy chair just screams to be used for reading. A table with fresh flowers or a bowl of cherries lights up the senses. It's the little things that create a space for flow and light that spark of joy for learning.

How you organize your space – whether big or small – lays the foundation for your homeschool. The design is based entirely on how you want your children to learn. A space for traditional homeschoolers will look much different than that of a roadschooler.

It will also vary based on age. A space for young preschoolers will look much different compared to that of late elementary learners. Or, if you have a blend of ages, that could look different, too.

You also want to consider the size of your space. No one says you need an entire room. When we lived in a townhouse, we used a small section of our small living room to learn. You can use the kitchen table, the couch, the bed, really anywhere. Learning doesn't have to be at a desk; it can be anywhere in the home or even in the world.

Homeschool By Design means you get to create your space as you see fit. You get to create a space that works for your home environment and how your kids learn best. It doesn't have to be a room. It can be a shelf, baskets, a wall, or any space that can be designated to holding your homeschool things.

To start organizing your space, you want to first decide where the space is actually located. If you aren't sure where you want your homeschool space to be, pay attention to where you spend the most time in the house.

Is it the basement?

Is it the kitchen?

Is it the living room?

Is it a bedroom?

Maybe you don't want the learning space anywhere near the TV due to distractions. Or perhaps you want it in the room with the TV so it can be used to support lessons with YouTube videos. Ask yourself the questions and decide where you want to keep your homeschool space.

Design the Space

Now that you have an area in mind, next comes the actual design of it. Consider the following questions.

Do you want to have things on the wall? Like a map or a bulletin board?

Do you want a place to hang art projects?

Is there a table in the space? Will you need to get one? Do you even want one?

Do you want shelving in the space?

Should things be set up lower for younger kids? Higher for older kids? A bit of both?

Do you want to include a space to call your own?

Do you want to have one space for organizing your materials and one space for the actual sit-down learning? If so, how will that look?

Do you plan to travel/roadschool/worldschool? If so, what are the most important things to have with you?

Lots to consider here. Also, remember the space will change as your children grow. What you set in place now can be switched up later, so try not to panic. You're not building anything permanent, just coming up with your desired design. It's your space, how you want, which works best for your family's needs.

Baskets and Mason Jars Make a House a Home

I know I'm not the only basket and mason jar-obsessed mama. If you fit into this category, you are my people! Louie used to call me the basket lady. I collected all the baskets from every thrift store and garage sale in case I could use them somewhere in our homeschool.

Baskets are amazing to store things in when you're organizing, especially for the younger ones. Blocks, books, peg dolls, shapes, science materials, pretty much everything could be stored in a pretty basket. Line them all up on the shelves, and you're set!

Mason jars are also fantastic. Pom-poms, pipe cleaners, folded felt pieces, stamps, special markers, paintbrushes, scissors, freshly sharpened pencils. These all fit the bill for the mason jar storage.

As my boys have grown, I've let go of most of my baskets since they are not much use for us anymore (insert crying emoji here). We use a small caddy that holds pencils, erasers, markers, glue, and scissors. It's not often we need more than this. Despite my heartbreak of letting go of so many baskets, you might still find them carrying chalk, rock collections, and fruit in various places around my house.

<u>Organizing Shelves and Bins</u>

Shelves are my besties. We have 19 shelves in this house, varying in sizes and colors (thank you, Ikea!). They mostly hold the ginormous book collection we have, which I swear I purge every year, but more books just seem to crawl their way into my shopping cart anytime I pass them by.

Shelves are so simple to put together and very versatile. Aside from the apparent use of holding books, they can be used to display individual activities in baskets, to store board games, or to display a project. They can be used for categorizing topics for learning, to line up unique teacups for poetry tea time, or as a place for your cat to take a nap. So very versatile.

For filling your shelf, make a plan. Will you be using a lot of Montessori activities and require each shelf to have a tray of materials? Or maybe you want to have a shelf for each child with a bin to hold all their work.

I used to use magazine bins on our shelves to keep the boys' workbooks and various curriculums organized on the shelves. So helpful and easily labeled.

Take the ideas above and make a plan for your shelves and how you want to organize them.

Make room for a shelf, even a small one. You won't regret it.

Another object I would highly recommend is a 4 to 10-drawer organization chest on wheels. These drawers are where you'll store:

- lined paper
- construction paper
- extra pencils, markers, pencil crayons, or crayons
- craft supplies
- paint
- felt board and felt pieces
- magnetic board and pieces
- glue and tape
- ropes, strings, ribbons, popsicle sticks
- readers
- extra journals or notebooks
- approved grab-and-go snacks
- all the items you use to document learning

Anything that doesn't fit or look right on the shelves can be stored in one of these organization chests. They help keep the clutter down, and the top of the bin can be used to store mason jars or a basket of toys.

Tips for Organizing

Use what you've got. Do you have a coffee table with a little shelf underneath? Amazing! Because that shelf can hold a few plastic bins with so many homeschool materials, like a bin with crayons, coloring books, lego, reading books, workbooks. This list could go on forever. Check around your home for items you can use.

Use organizational tools. Bins, baskets, containers, and mason jars are all great ways to keep your homeschool tools organized.

Don't like it? Switch it up! If you've been homeschooling from a space that just doesn't feel right or look right or it's distracting somehow, change things. This is your design, so make it fit just right.

Everything has a place. This Montessori saying *'A place for everything and everything in its place'* should really be a life goal. When everything has a home, you're a well-organized mama. If something has no place, you may have too many things. Too many things equal clutter. Too much clutter equals an overwhelmed brain and lack of focus. A good rule of thumb is if something has no place, it's time to donate or donate something else to make room for the item.

Keep up with de-cluttering. Like the message above, clutter causes overwhelm. To keep the clutter to a minimum, do a weekly or monthly purge of the things no longer necessary. If the kids are done that project that's been on the shelf for two months, take pictures of it and let it go (with their permission, of course).

Label everything. Louie bought me a label maker once, and I was the happiest person ever. Labeling things is such fun for an organizing junkie! It keeps everything well organized. It lets the kids know where to find items, and helps with the little ones learning how to read. We've even labeled things in other languages to help it stick.

It's the Small Things

Think of these two scenarios:

Scenario 1: The kids sit at the table dotted with crumbs and dried pasta sauce from last night's dinner. There are water glasses left on it, half-filled, and 3 toys Mom pulled off from the floor.

Scenario 2: The kids sit at the clean table with a bowl of floating candles, lit, and a mini vase of tulips.

If you were to sit down and be ready to learn which table would you prefer? Consider this thought every time you prepare the space for your children to learn.

Some small things you can do to make your learning space inviting:
* set up little bowls of snacks (nuts are our go-to)
* have meditative music playing
* add a vase with aromatic flowers or herbs
* put on a diffuser with essential oils that support focus, such as Peppermint or Wild Orange
* light candles with an intention for great homeschool moments
* clear out clutter

You have your space designed, your shelves planned, and all the organization materials listed that you need. You know how to add small, but special, things into your space to make it more inviting. What missing? Oh yes, *what* to put in that space. Let's take a gander over to Tools of the Trade.

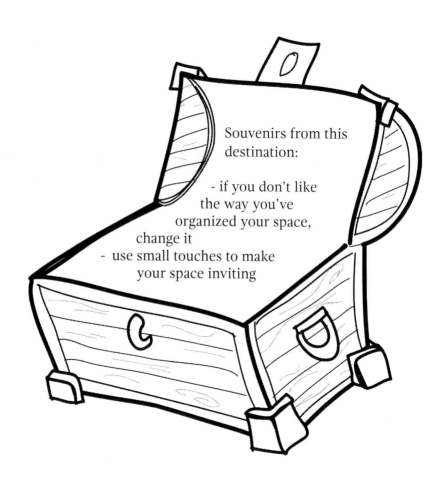

Souvenirs from this destination:

- if you don't like the way you've organized your space, change it
- use small touches to make your space inviting

What you need

ONCE YOU HAVE your curriculum set and your space ready to go, you need some tools to go along with them.

Do you remember the stationary store flyers coming just before the start of the school season? And you'd grab a highlighter, go through all the pages, and highlight all the items you *must* have for the new school year? Wasn't that thrilling?

Or maybe it's just me.

Either way, gathering the tools for your homeschool is the same sort of fun. Imagine your kiddos using those newly sharpened pencils, cracking open that new stack of construction paper, and not needing to pry off old glue from a new set of glue bottles. Lovely!

Give Me A List

I've had this request a lot from people. *Can you give me a list of everything I'll need?* Need and want are two different things. Need: paper and a pencil. Want: all the other stuff, plus chocolate.

Depending on your budget, you may want to purchase items over time. Maybe there's one big item on your wish list, like a telescope. Perhaps that big purchase can be for an end-of-the-year celebratory moment instead of all-at-once when you start. It's your design, you get to choose what to get and when.

Here's my general list in no particular order and for various ages:

Perfect to start:

- Pencils: Lots of them. While you're at it, grab a decent sharpener.

- Erasers: White ones are best because they don't smear like all the others.

- Lined paper: If you're using workbooks, you might not think you need lined paper, but you do. Excellent for working out math problems, for using out in nature when observing critters, and making paper airplanes.

- Pencil crayons or crayons: You need a coloring tool! Purchase name brands because the dollar store ones suck.
- Glue: Buy both liquid and stick versions, again a name brand to ensure quality.

- Scissors: Start with kid-sized ones and work your way up over the years. Always have extras. Scissors are like socks in a dryer; they hide when you need them.

- Binders: To collect all the loose worksheets and other work.

- Notebooks: To use for writing, spelling, or doodling.

Then you can add:

- White printer paper: Lots. Buy one big box for the year and see where that takes you.

- Play-dough, clay, plasticine: These are excellent learning tools for all ages! From young ones using it to form shapes to older ones using plasticine to build a model of the Colosseum.

- 3-holed punch: You'll be doing a lot of hole punching.

- Popsicle sticks: The use of popsicle sticks are endless and for every age. Young ones can use them as counters; older ones can use them to design catapults.

- Pom poms: For crafts or to use for sorting by color or size.
- Glue gun: When regular glue just won't do. Get the glue gun sticks, too.

- Markers: Because it's fun to have more than one coloring tool.

- Construction paper: For crafts, art, and so many other projects.

- Oil pastels: They are more vibrant than crayons and color so smoothly. It's a fun experiment to notice the difference between these and crayons.

- Paintbrushes: Obvious choice – you need these to paint!

- Tempra paint: From babies to early elementary, these are great for finger paints or regular painting. Bonus: they easily wash off.

- Acrylic paint: For older children ready to take painting to the next level.

- Watercolors: Younger children can enjoy the mixing of watercolors, but older children can really learn techniques, like blending.

- Extra journals: You just never know when someone needs a journal.

- Small pads of paper: Great for quick note-taking, solving math problems, and taking on an adventure with you.

- Sticky notes: Use these to help with documenting, writing the kids' questions on them, and mark pages in workbooks or books you read.

- Tape: Every kind. You won't regret it.

- Clipboards: Get a few of these. You'll notice you use them often when going outside or when doing work inside a fort.

- Sketchbooks: The dollar store is an excellent source for these. We love them for YouTube art classes and drawing tutorials.

- Mini whiteboard: One for each child is perfect to use for working out things like math problems.

- Whiteboard markers: One set for each child to go with their whiteboard.

Great additions:

- Bulletin board: Large or small, they are perfect for hanging a calendar, a map, kid's work, your schedule, etc.

- Calendar: If you choose to incorporate the daily calendar for younger ones, a wall calendar is perfect. For older ones, an agenda works well.

- Magnetic letters and numbers: For the littles who are learning. Also, grab a metal cookie sheet to use as a portable magnetic board.

- Wall map: It's so useful to have this to find locations.

Wish list:

- Laser color printer: super helpful for projects or activities that really need color.

- Tablets or laptops: Using one family computer or tablet can be tricky. If you can manage it, having one for each child, or at least more than one for the whole family, splurge! It's totally worth it, especially if you have multiple children.

- Whiteboard or blackboard: If your space offers it, a whiteboard or blackboard is perfect for lessons. If you decide on the blackboard, grab chalk, too.

- Laminator: These are quite reasonable in price. I laminated so much when the boys were younger, and my laminator was worth it times 100. Better than the crazy costs of laminating at the stationary stores.

- Bookbinding machine: Another item that's not as expensive as you think, these machines are like magnets to kids. If a child doesn't want to write a book, show them this machine, and they'll be writing in no time. Who wouldn't want a book of potty poems bound?

- Microscope: We started with a cheap (maybe $15) microscope that attaches to my phone and uses the phone's camera to see small things. It's not amazing, but it works for now. Pretty soon, we'll be getting the real thing.

Morning Rhythm

When they were little wee ones, we had a morning rhythm after breakfast that would lead our learning time. I had a big basket (obviously) that was filled with the items we were currently learning. Things like matching cards, the book we would read, a mini felt board with felt letters and numbers, finger puppets, and anything else appropriate to their stage for learning.

As a traditional homeschooler (when they were little), I wanted to keep a similar style of learning they would receive in school. So I would sing the songs and read the books, me sitting on a rocking chair and them on the floor. There was something so comforting to me about that. Familiarity, maybe?

Proper:

If you have a vision for your homeschool to include such a rhythm, you'll definitely want these supplies on your 'need' list:

- Bulletin board: You can find these at office stores and mini versions from dollar stores. Garage sales and online marketplaces are also great places to find one.

- Calendar: Grab one from the local dollar store along with the months of the year and numbers for the calendar

- Felt board: You can make one of these easily with cardboard and a piece of felt. Then purchase felt numbers, letters, or print them out and glue felt to the back to use on your board.

As the boys grew up, the basket and morning rhythm grew up with them. Instead of using a bulletin board, calendar, and felt board, we used:

- Mad libs: I remember these as a kid not as a learning tool, but as a fun game. Turns out, there's a lot of grammar and vocabulary to learn.

- A word-of-the-day calendar: Because I would get a kick out of the times Cruz would say things like 'bioluminescent' when he was three. So cute!

- Word search and crossword books: These offer more vocabulary skills, problem-solving, and spelling. Found all over dollar stores, these can be replaced cheaply once completed.

- Journals for free writing: As a self-admitted journal junkie, I hope to pass this trait down to the boys. Seriously, though, these are perfect for jotting down plans to find out if we really do have a monster in the basement.

Time to check yourself. You have your list of needed and wanted supplies for your space and maybe even a bit of an idea for using your tools in a morning rhythm. You're all done here – next stop, how to home-school on a budget.

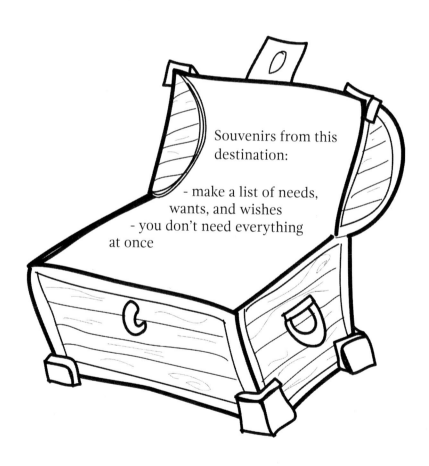

Souvenirs from this destination:

- make a list of needs, wants, and wishes
- you don't need everything at once

Get the most for your money

I'M SERIOUS WHEN I tell you that there's never been a more excellent time in history to homeschool your kids on a budget. The amount of free information out there is almost too much to handle! In fact, I went to school to teach, not to be an entrepreneur. Never once did I take any sort of business course or anything. I literally taught myself via Google search and have built pretty big businesses since jumping into this lifestyle in 2005.

I joke with my kids about not going to university or college but instead spending the money on starting their own business or interning someplace they love. But am I joking? Hrmm...

Anyways, back to the budget thing. We literally had zero money when we had Cruz. 'Tis the life of the entrepreneur – we were growing our businesses. Despite being in all sorts of debt back then (which I won't disclose because my parents might die of shock), I was able to pull it together and find various free, or relatively cheap, ways to educate the boys. In those early years, we might have spent $100-$200 on homeschooling things for the *entire* year of materials because we just couldn't pull off much more than that. So let me tell you, you can absolutely homeschool your children on a tight budget.

Check your satchel for your Deal Glasses. Use these when you're looking for a deal. I've had these on my whole life because my parents taught me the thrill of finding something on sale or priced in one place better than another. If there was a deal to be found, I would be the one to find it. These glasses helped me immensely when our budget was teeny tiny.

All the Free Things

Pinterest

You could spend hours finding free ideas, activities, and printables on Pinterest. My biggest tip is to create different Pinterest boards for various homeschool topics. For example, homeschool art, homeschool science, homeschool lego, homeschool math, etc. Take a half-hour each day and add to one of those topics, searching for free things. If it's toddler math ideas, type in "free toddler math." If it's grade 5 body systems, type in "free grade 5 body systems" and go nuts! Pin all the things you find helpful or interesting and want to save for later or use in a future lesson.

TeachersPayTeachers.com

Although this site is designed for traditional school teachers, you'll find a lot of resources you can use with your kids. Let's say its Halloween, and you're looking for a math riddle, just type 'Halloween math' in the search bar and choose the filter for 'age' and 'free.' Using freebies from teachers on this platform led me to find some of our favorite activities, which led to further purchase from these teachers/homeschoolers. It's great to support fellow educators!

The Library

You can't get any better than accessing free books and programs. Use your local library to your advantage. The staff can even help with resources you may be looking for if they don't have it. They are well versed in all things within the community and can provide lots of guidance.

Borrow From Friends

Connect with other homeschoolers and see if you can swap resources. If you have a big bin of science materials and a friend has one of art, why not trade for a couple of weeks? You not only get access to free materials, but also you are giving that same opportunity to another family.

Team Up

Do you have to teach math and don't want to? Are you great at art? Find another homeschooler, team up, and swap lessons! You can teach everyone art, and they can teach everyone math. Teaming up with other homeschoolers is great for your sanity and also allows you to share your strength and passion with kids who aren't your own. It's incredible how great other people's kids are to teach. They just appreciate your coolness so much more than your own kiddos.

YouTube

This has been the biggest saving grace in our homeschool! No matter what you are teaching, I can almost guarantee you can find something relating to that topic on YouTube. From science experiments to beginner art classes to writing persuasive paragraphs to learning the alphabet, it's all there.

My boys use it, especially for gaming. They learn a lot of tips and tricks to get better at their games. They don't realize how much they learn when they hop on to research these kinds of things! Shh...do not tell them I said that.

Here's a list of some excellent YouTube channels:

- Art for Kids Hub: He's such a great teacher. He takes things step-by-step, walking kids through drawing. He even includes all the most popular characters from kid movies and shows.
-
- Cosmic Kids Yoga: The stories she uses to walk kids through a yoga class is fantastic. She also has meditations to calm those active minds.
-
- Operation Ouch: Created by twin doctors, they cover incredible facts about the body. Funny and informative, your kids would be happy to watch these for fun!
-
- Sesame Street: It was good for us as kids, and it's still great for youngins today.
-
- Lego: Keeping it creative and encouraging builds, this channel even includes lessons with stop-animation.

Fine print: YouTube is terrific, but it can some-times be like the wild, wild west in terms of content. As a parent, be sure the material is appropriate for them and their level of learning. Only you know this!

Budget-Friendly Purchases

If you're looking to purchase items, materials, or curriculum on a budget, these are easy ways to save on purchases.

Dollar stores: I really don't need to go far into this one. We all know that dollar stores provide every crafting resource you'll need – all the paper, pencils, erasers, binders, craft supplies, counters, everything.

Thrift shops: Oh, the baskets! And the books! Every trip to the thrift shop brings joy because you never know what you will find. You'll likely come out with so much more than you expected. Our favorite things to purchase at thrift shops are books, board games, and crafting material.

Garage sales: I could go on forever on garage sales. Not only can you find anything and everything to use in your homeschool, but you get to teach your children about money and the art of negotiation. This is some-thing I'm the worst at, but Louie is the best. We would have mock conversations in the car on how to negotiate for something, and the boys would practice when they found something at a garage sale they wanted to buy. Perfect.

Ikea: If you're looking for child-sized tables, easels, or painting paper, this is the best budget-friendly spot. For less than $50, you can pick up those more significant purchases that will last for years to come.

Used book stores: Books are crucial to learning, and sometimes we just want our own copy instead of something from the library. This is especially true if you are using a literature-based homeschool curriculum and want a book for your collection.

Amazon: If you're not able to find the used books you need from the thrift shop of a used book store, this is the place to check. You can also grab reasonably priced curriculum workbooks if you plan to use them.

Homeschool sales: Every year in spring and summer, you'll find homeschool curriculum sales and bundle sales. This is a great time to purchase if you're looking for a specific curriculum and sticking to a budget. Sales also pop up during other times of the year, but spring/summer seems to be the most active time. You can find these sales through your local homeschool community or online by joining the newsletters of the curriculum you're interested in purchasing.

How to Budget

I used to feel really guilty about money. When it came to spending on homeschooling, that guilt was magnified because I thought I needed the best of the best if I wanted my boys to have any chance in life. Those 'best' would cost an arm and a leg.

Eventually, I learned that what I viewed as 'best' didn't mean best for my boys.

I also learned a technique. At the beginning of the month, you designate your money by telling it where to go. For example, I made a list of expected income and then assigned that to bills, food, car stuff, emergencies, savings, and homeschooling. This changed my life.

When I knew I had money that was specific for homeschooling, those guilty feelings went away. The money *had* to be used for homeschooling materials. There was no other use for it. In my mind, the money was already deposited into the invisible homeschool account. The guilt was gone. Hooray!

This is how we budgeted our homeschool. From there, I knew what I could expect each month to be spent on the materials we needed. I always designated more money in the spring/summer for the curriculum sales (oh yes, keep your eyes peeled for those) and around the holidays for more deals.

If our budget didn't offer enough for a more significant purchase we wanted, we would find a way to bring in more income. As Louie has always said: *don't budget, make more.* I'm not telling you to follow his mantra, but think about some simple ways to bring in a few extra bucks. Holding a garage sale could earn enough for your entire year's worth of homeschool expenses. Plus, you'd declutter a whole lot and make room for your special space. Bonus!

We've come so far, homeschoolers (I'm calling you that now)! But we aren't done yet. We've got two more islands to cover. Let's head to **All About You Island** next!

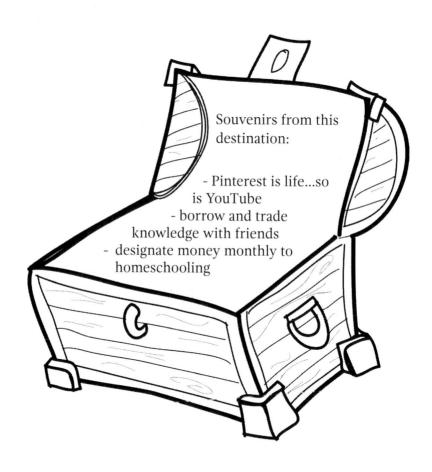

Souvenirs from this destination:

- Pinterest is life...so is YouTube
- borrow and trade knowledge with friends
- designate money monthly to homeschooling

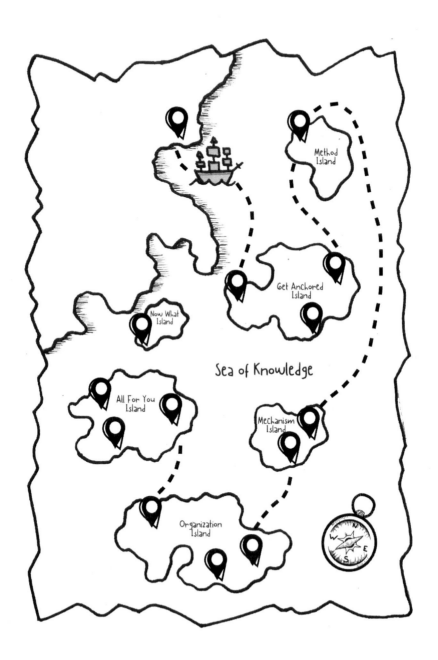

Doing things for you

WELCOME TO THE island! Our first destination is **Self Love**. We can't lead our families in learning without being our best first. That means digging deep into patterns and thoughts – shadow work, we can call it.

Sounds scary? It's not! It's freeing when we look at the patterns we don't realize we have. The parts of us that hid in the shadows. Bringing some light onto them allows us to recognize them and grow. That's the whole point, right? We can't expect our kiddos to learn and grow without us doing the same.

I have a project for you before we get into this first destination. Ready?

Go look in the mirror and say these words: I love you.

Bet that felt awkward, right? If not, then you've been doing some fine work on yourself!

This may seem out of context for a homeschool book, but listen up...Self-love doesn't just mean taking baths and time for yourself. It also means taking the time to grow and become a better version of yourself. A shift needs to be made not only in the way we take care of ourselves in our bodies but also in our minds.

You want to be at your best. When you are leading the family and are at your best in mind, body, and spirit, you set the energy for the rest of the members. From the standpoint of an empath (both myself and Avery), when one person in the house is upset, it totally affects the rest of us! Not to say we can't be angry or to brush off high strung emotions, quite the opposite, but we work through them and don't let them fester.

This is an act of self-love. And it reverberates throughout our entire home.

Therefore, I declare it to be of grand importance to improve the love of ourselves as we design our homeschools. Do I sound like the queen? That was me trying to sound like the queen.

We need to be loving ourselves a bit more. Let's do that with our minds.

Tricks We Play

Our brain is a pretty remarkable three pounds. It runs all our subconscious body systems, makes sure we gather nutrients we need for our bodies to develop and grow and tricks us into thinking things that aren't true.

Our brains are ancient. As cave people, we were always on high alert for danger. If we weren't, we'd be eaten by something in about 5 seconds. It's no wonder it's still trying to protect us. Aww, thanks, brain.

These influences still ring true, and our brains continue to look for danger, hundreds of thousands of years later. One way it does this is by telling us stories. We believe them because, well, our brain told us so. It's sifting through thousands of things happening around us every second, telling us what's important and what's not. So when it tells us we aren't good enough, we believe it. These stories often come from childhood experiences, but I'll leave that talk for the therapist.

Change the Self-Talk

Self-talk is the official name of our brain telling us things. It can be negative (you aren't good enough) or positive (listen up...you are a rockstar). A part of self-love is managing these negative thought patterns and claiming neutral ground or bringing through more positive thoughts.

Negative self-talk that revolves around homeschooling can be:
* I'm not good enough to be doing this.
* I don't know enough to teach the kids.
* We don't have enough money to homeschool.

To change how we feel about something, we've got to change the way we think about it. If we believe we aren't good enough to homeschool, we need to change the way we think about it.

If we are free-flowing, creative types and our image of homeschooling is that of a strict, rule-following family, of course, we won't feel good enough.

If we imagine teaching grade 12 chemistry and don't know what the symbol is for Mercury, of course, we won't feel we know enough to teach the kids.

If we are on a tight budget and we see curriculum costs are in the hundreds, of course, we feel we don't have enough money.

Grab your satchel and pull out some of the examples of negative self-talk you have wrapped up around homeschooling. Let's change the way we think about these things instead.

Perhaps you find you think: *I'm not good enough to be doing this.* Re-write it as: *I love my kids, and that's enough to be able to design a homeschool that is perfect for our family.*

Or maybe its: *I don't know enough to teach the kids.* Re-write it as: *I know plenty, and if/when we need support, there's an entire internet out there to answer questions I cannot answer.*

It might even be: *We don't have enough money to homeschool.* Re-write it as: *We have a small budget for homeschooling that will offer more than enough for our needs.*

By changing the way we think about something, we can change how we feel about it. Doesn't that feel so much better? Try a few more in your Field Guide with some negative self-talk that's been sprouting up in your head.

Stop Comparing. Stop It Right Now.

Comparison is a thief, a pirate trying to steal your kind thoughts about yourself on this journey. It is the thief of joy.

This is a common quote we see online, but it rings so true when it comes to homeschooling. So often we get caught in the trap of social media photos and perfect Instagram school rooms, and we wonder, *'how on earth am I doing this so wrong?'*

We judge ourselves, and we feel like our small spaces aren't good enough or that our bookshelves aren't full enough or that we don't have enough paint supplies to allow our children to be the best painters they can be in life.

Let me give you this one tip. If you take nothing else from this book, consider this: stop comparing yourself to others. Make the comparison thief walk the plank.

***

When the boys were in the early elementary age, Louie would wake up every morning to me, raising my voice to the boys. Every morning. They were not moving an inch when it came to getting work done, and I had hit my limit. It took me some time to realize it wasn't them not doing the work, it was me not taking care of myself.

I had these high expectations of what a 'perfect' home-schooler should look like, which was my expectation for myself. I saw these fantastic bloggers and social media influencers who, I believed, had homeschooling done right.

I was rigid, inflexible, and expected a lot of the boys, too. I expected them and myself to 'look the part' of the perfect homeschooler. To follow the set schedule and do the work just like they would if they were in traditional school. I often wondered how on earth those unschoolers could just let their kids be to run around with such flexibility when really that's what my heart was calling out the most.

I put all my time into these rigid schedules and worked every night on Pinterest to gather as many resources as I could to 'prove' (to whom I don't know!) that I was good enough. That I was just as amazing as those other home-schoolers, I followed.

Those patterns and stories I held so firmly about what a 'good enough' homeschooler looked like was ludicrous! I was ready to send my kids to school (gasp!) because of this, yet it was my own thought patterns and expectations. I wasn't caring enough about myself to let go of the compari-son thief.

I reflected on this and made changes over the next few weeks, and guess what? Those morning yell-fests never happened again.

***

The issue I had in this story was that of compar-ing myself to others. I put expectations on myself based on what I saw others doing. That darn comparison thief stole my joy again!

If we think hard about it, we are continually comparing ourselves to others to validate our own actions or choices. When we see people far ahead of where we are, the comparison thief really takes its toll. It's like we are spinning down a water funnel of negativity and shameful self-talk. We can't grab the safety rope to pull ourselves back out.

There are a few things we can do when we try to compare ourselves to others:

1. Remind ourselves that we are beginning our journey, and many of the people we compare ourselves to are in the middle or end of their homeschool journey. We cannot compare our beginning to someone else middle or end! It's like saying – *Sheesh...this beginner's painting class I took sure isn't anything like the Mona Lisa.* Yeah, no kidding! But I bet if you kept painting for years and honing that skill, you'd find your own fabulous style and be better than any museum offers! Accept that you are at the beginning stage and know that it's enough.

2. Practice gratitude. I know it's overdone. But still, this is a great way to look at it. Focus on what you do have and how far you've come. Like, hey! You're reading this book right now so you can better prepare yourself for the decision of homeschooling! That's something to be proud of and grateful for, right? It's better than Betty down the street who keeps complaining about the school system but doesn't take action.

3. Unfollow the triggers. That's right, stop following the people that are so far down their path that you envy them. Instead, stay in your own lane and focus on where you are going.

4. Take action. When you compare yourself, recognize that it's only harmful if it becomes obsessive or af-

fects your life. If someone has something you want or desire to achieve, make it into a goal and start the steps to get you there.

You know who you can compare yourself to? Yourself. From like 5 minutes ago. Do you know more now than you did 5 minutes ago? Can you be better? Yep.

Now that's a great comparison. You've walked the thief off the plank.

Building Boundaries

When I was twenty, I saw a therapist for a generalized anxiety disorder. One of the first things she did was tell me to read the book Boundaries by Dr. Henry Cloud and Dr. John Townsend. I could never have imagined such a concept! Boundaries? You mean I don't have to do things because people manipulated me in a way I felt forced to or the guilt was too much for me to bear? Huh.

Boundaries sound restrictive, but that's towards the person crossing them. For you, they are freeing!

Let's say you're on a call with a friend and your child comes up to you screaming 'Mommy, Mommy, Mommy' until you tell your friend you need to call her back because your child wants something. Turns out, they wanted you to find a toy on the shelf for them.

Having proper boundaries will teach your kiddos to wait their turn or help themselves in such a situation. We taught our boys from when they were around three and four that if we were ever on the phone, they could come over and hold our hand. I would squeeze it to let them know *I know* they need something. They would then wait until I had a pause in my conversation or until I got off the phone until they asked their question.

This didn't happen right away, so don't be thinking 'that will never happen' because I thought the same thing when my mom offered this suggestion from some article she read. I taught this to the boys in steps.

First, we practiced this technique when I was on the phone with my mom. Then, we practiced when I was on the phone with others in my family. It took a week or two, but they figured it out, and that boundary was set.

Setting boundaries with your kids gives you some freedom, is an act of self-love, and teaches those kiddos to respect someone else's space. Make a list of the areas you could use boundaries with your kids (hey, no barging in when Mom's on the toilet!) and start setting them.

Boundaries don't just work for kids, but for anyone else in your life. If you have a friend who's always calling you with the latest drama and pulling you away from more important things, it's time to set a boundary. If you have a family member always expecting you to watch her children on a whim, it's time to set a boundary. Embrace the word no. Practice saying it as confidently as your kids say it when you tell them to eat broccoli.

Stop Should-ing Yourself

I should put my kids in sports.

I should have taught them this by now.
I should have a strict schedule in place.
I should have a nicer space for them to learn.
I should have more toys.
I should have fewer toys.
I should teach during regular school times.
I should make them read on their own.
I should force them to do the work their peers are be doing.
I should be enjoying this more.
I should have a more organized space.
I should get the kids out of their PJs.
I should I should I should.

Eww. Just reading that gives me heart palpitations. Can we make a pact to stop should-ing ourselves? It's only another version of our brains telling us we aren't good enough.

Instead, let's change our *shoulds* into *wants*. Look how different this list looks now.

I want to put my kids in sports.
I want to teach them this.
I want to have a strict schedule in place.
I want to have a nicer space for them to learn.
I want to have more toys.
I want to have fewer toys.
I want to teach during regular school times.
I want them to read on their own.
I want them to do the work their peers are be doing.
I want to be enjoying this more.
I want to have a more organized space.
I want to get the kids out of their PJs.

See what's happening? You own it. Feels much better, doesn't it?

Be an Example

Have you ever heard the quote 'you are a sum of the 5 people you hang around with'? You become those people you're closest to. Consider this when thinking about your kids. Who are they around all the time?

It's you.

It's a big responsibility, but it's true. It's also the reason some of our children trigger us sometimes – they can be a perfect reflection of the things we don't like about ourselves. It's time we take this seriously.

If you're the kind of mama who puts everyone else's needs ahead of her own, guess what your kids will do when they are adults? They will take care of everyone else before themselves.

Now, I'm not saying we can't be giving and kind and caring. What I am saying is you need to include yourself in all the giving, kindness, and caring! Why do we have guilt about giving ourselves some me-time or doing something for ourselves before others?

Before you take off in a plane, they tell you what to do if the masks drop. That is, put *your* mask on and then help others. Why do they tell you this? Because you can help no one else if you've passed out.

Be an example to your kids. Take care of yourself, give yourself time for things you enjoy, and let them see you working on projects just for you. They will remember this. You are giving them permission to do the same – without guilt – when they grow to be adults.

Finding Your People

Part of loving yourself means surrounding yourself with people who care about you. Those people are such a gift! Early in my journey, I had such a strong desire to find homeschoolers like me, but it took me some time – and lots of attending various homeschool events – to find my people.

Aside from the obvious join-homeschool-groups option, you can also:
- Attend local homeschool events
- Join homeschool classes at museums, libraries, recreation centers, etc
- Sign your children up for homeschool spelling bees or science fairs where you can connect with other families
- Join a co-op in your area
- Register your child for a homeschool club (drama, science, lego, etc.)
- Visit parks during traditional school hours
- Publish an online ad or put up posters in the community asking to connect with other homeschoolers
- Check-in with your country's homeschool association and ask about groups

The Magic of Morning Rituals

There's something about morning rituals that just set your day off so perfectly. Another beautiful part about homeschooling (as you can tell, there are so many) is that you can wake up when you want to, start your day when you want, and it doesn't need to be rushed or forced or chaotic.

A routine can include sitting with a cup of tea and watching rabbits in the backyard nibbling away at the freshly cut grass. It can be the children doing their morning routine, jumping on the mini-trampoline to get some exercise before they start their day.

It could be gathering around the counter, making breakfast together in the morning, and taking supplements to make their bodies healthy as they grow into little adults.

A routine can also look like taking the time to sit and be – whether in meditation or a calming yoga pose, sending kind thoughts out to set up the rest of your day. Having morning rituals is like taking a deep, slow breath. It brings calm and peaceful reflection and joy and then leads into the rest of your day.

If you don't already have a morning ritual, I encourage you to find something that fits for you and for your family. But most especially for you. You are the caretaker, the gatekeeper of your family. You are the most critical person to pour into every day. This allows it to be at your very best for your family, and when you're at your best, life flows so smoothly.

Take morning rituals for yourself. Get up an hour earlier and do the things that light up your soul. For me, this often looks like writing, learning about herbalism, or tarot. Those are the things that are part of me.

What are the things that are a part of you? What lifts you up? What lifts you up so much that you'd be willing to get up a whole hour earlier than the rest of the family in the house? Because that thing is worth it. It's worth you doing.

Maybe you love art or drawing or reading. Maybe love to bake or cook or to work out. There is no right answer here; it's whatever lights you up whatever brings you peace.

I challenge you to spend the next week getting up a bit earlier than everyone else. Take the time to do the thing that lights up your soul. Create your magical morning ritual. You'll see pretty quickly how beautiful your days are when you start off focusing entirely on you.

From there, you build this onto the children and their magical rituals. What lights them up, and what makes them feel cozy and warm and loved? Have this be added to their morning.

Maybe they have a favorite cartoon and want to snuggle with you on the couch and watch it.

Maybe they want to rock in a chair with you and listen to you read to them. That could be their idea of connection and love. For them, it could be the perfect way to start their day.

That's the purpose of these magical rituals. They're meant to include a feeling of warmth, coziness, and love.

A word to the ones whose children are up early. I hear you, I genuinely do! This was me for a while. We learned to adjust our children's routine to give me the time I needed in the morning. If you think that's not possible, take a little one to Italy and watch how quickly they adjust to a new time schedule.

Maybe instead of your children going to bed at seven, they go to bed at nine. Instead of waking up at six, they wake up at eight. This little adjustment allows you to have that vital time to yourself in the morning. That's some self-love, right there.

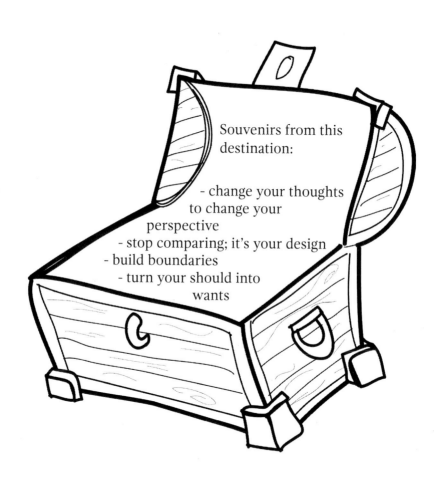

Souvenirs from this destination:

- change your thoughts to change your perspective
- stop comparing; it's your design
- build boundaries
- turn your should into wants

You can do both

SOME OF YOU may not require this destination, and that's fine. Move onto the next! Take only what you need from this quest.

My experience in working from home and homeschooling is vast, as I worked for myself from home throughout both my pregnancies, during infant stages and throughout their entire lives. I get it, I understand your struggles, because working from home has been a part of our homeschool life from day one.

The beauty of working from home is that you can shift your homeschool hours based on your work schedule, or vice versa.

When they were babies, I would work from their bedtime at 7 pm until the first feed of the night, which was 1 am. Then I'd crash for the night and do it all over again. Naps were a dream because I could make any calls during nap time that couldn't happen in my night shift.

Once naps were gone, I stuck to my nighttime routine. During the day, I'd take them to meetings or visit the venue for my next event.

As soon as they could speak in full sentences, they grew into little helpers for my businesses. They would help me put posters up for my shows, deliver flyers, help with set up, etc. They've been brought up into a world of entrepreneurial spirit. To see them now, it makes sense why they are who they are. Their environment has shaped them over the years.

In fact, just last year at my vegan food festival, they ran the merchandise table all on their own! At 8 and 10 years old. It's all they've ever known since they've taken part in it every year since its inception in 2012.

Working from home means you can include your children in your work if you want to. Let them organize something for you or design something for you. Ask them to help you brainstorm on a topic or an idea. They'll learn responsibility, expectations, and what it's like to do adult-type work.

Do you remember being a kid and wondering what your parents did all day at work? I know I did. I loved going to work with my mom over holiday breaks, where I could care for the kids at the shelter where she worked. I got a glimpse into her world and felt like a little adult when I got to help. Give your kids that chance!

Now maybe incorporating them into your work *doesn't* work. Read on, homeschooler.

How Do You Work and Homeschool?

As I mentioned, I was an entrepreneur before having kiddos, so when they were born, I never even took a maternity leave. When Avery was one-and-a-half and Cruz was 2 months old, I was producing a consumer trade show. Cruz, as a newborn, was strapped to me for the entire 4 days of set-up and the show so I could breastfeed him on demand. Luckily it was a *baby* consumer show, so it was totally appropriate. But just know, *I get you!*

I get what it's like to work from home (and be on-site) when you've got babies at home. And then toddlers, preschoolers, and elementary ages at home. I understand how hard it is to balance your work life and family life when your kids are fighting, and you have the most important phone call. I know the fears and the tears when it all seems too much or when it all seems to fall apart.

Now that mine are at an age where they can care for themselves, it's *way* easier to work from home. However, for those harder years (or, you know, when the kids won't stop fighting or won't release themselves from your leg), I have a few tips for you:

- **Set reasonable expectations.** Your children won't be able to occupy themselves for 4 straight hours while you work. Instead, break it down into more manageable times. Perhaps you have emails to respond to – let your kids watch a TV show and set a timer for yourself to get the emails done. You'll be *amazed* how efficient you can be in communicating when you know you have a timed deadline!

- **Put your phone on airplane mode.** This trick works wonders with the timer tips from above. You really must try it. It's the simplest thing to do, and if you typically get distracted by any phone ding or vibration, you'll find this to be game-changing. When you need to get that quick work done, put your phone on airplane mode and get to it.

- **Break things up.** This goes along with the first two. Breaking up your day into chunks of work time is so helpful for both you and your kids. They get your attention, and then you get work time.

- **Take advantage of nap times.** I did my best work in the hour-long naps my kids would take. As I said, there's something about being efficient when you know you only have a small window of time to do stuff.

- **Roll with it.** Sometimes, the kids need more of your attention. Maybe they are sick or needing emotional support. That may mean you work later than you'd like. Keep your focus on them first. If they need their mom or dad, that comes before all other things. Work can be done later. Make sure they know this.

- **Take turns.** If you have a partner at home, take turns having fun with the kids. While they play, you work and vice versa.

- **Let them know how to reach you.** Before you have your designated work time while your kids play Minecraft, let them know the rules. "No knocking on the door unless it's an emergency "...and tell them the list of emergencies. Let them know there are consequences if they walk into your space, asking why their mod isn't working.

- **Hold their hand.** Remember learning this from the last destination? That self-love boundary thing? This worked so well when my boys were small and really taught them patience. If I were on a call with someone and they wanted/needed something, they would hold my hand. That let me know they had something they needed. I would squeeze their hand to let them know I understood they needed me, and they would either wait there while I finished my conversation or go back to what they were doing, knowing I would come to them in a moment. We practiced this a lot with grandma on the phone before I ever attempted it while I had business peeps on the phone!

- **Make a list.** This was a helpful thing for me as soon as the boys could read. I created a list of approved things to do while I was working. However, if I had to get on a call and could not be interrupted, it included a lot of screen time options. #noshame #no-judgement

- **Working more doesn't mean working well.** Learn how to manage your time by watching YouTube videos on things like the Pomodoro technique and other efficient working-type topics. You can do so much more in 15 minutes than you think you can.

- **Stop scrolling.** Social media is an addiction. BUT, we all want to lighten our days by checking out the latest memes that make us laugh. If you feel the need to scroll, set a timer for 5-10 minutes (I love timers) and scroll all you want. When that timer goes off, you're done. Get back to work. Better yet, if you're going to scroll productively, scroll through Pinterest, and pin all the great homeschool ideas.

- **Be grateful.** Many people wish they could homeschool, but cannot afford to lose the income they bring in or don't have a flexible work option that allows them to homeschool. Working from home is a blessing!

- **Plan meals.** Planning your meals for the week on Saturdays and grocery shopping on Sundays will make your weeks so much easier. You don't have to think once about what's for dinner. Plus, you can write it down for the kids to see, so they stop asking you the same question every day, *"what's for dinner?"*

- **Schedule you-time.** Working and homeschooling take a lot of energy. You're giving yourself to your kids full time plus more into your work. That's a lot of emptying of your cup. Spend time filling it up as well. Not only will it be beneficial for your sanity, but it also teaches your children to fill their own cups. You value yourself, which means your children will value themselves.

- **Delegate chores.** Children can start doing chores as young as two years old; you just need to set that expectation. If they play with something, they clean it up. If they spill something, they clean it up. As they get older, delegate chores based on their abilities. Check Pinterest for chore lists based on age and get to delegating. You aren't responsible for all the tasks.

- **Homeschool around work.** Maybe you don't work from home, perhaps you have to go to work. Here, design your homeschool to take place around your work schedule.

What does your dream work-and-homeschool day look like? Do that! Homeschooling can happen at any time – weekdays, weeknights, or weekends. It's part of the joy of your own design. Delegate the hard stuff, find simpler ways to manage household things, and hire out if you can. I am proof that working and homeschooling can absolutely happen at the same time. I couldn't join you here in this quest if it wasn't.

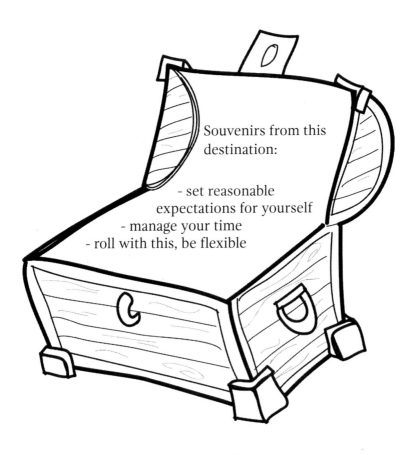

Souvenirs from this destination:

- set reasonable expectations for yourself
- manage your time
- roll with this, be flexible

Let's get them answered

WELCOME TO *Common Homeschool Questions*. I'm sure you have about a thousand as we close this quest, so let's see what I can do to answer the most common ones.

How long do I teach in a day?

This question often comes up for new home-schoolers, and it's an important one to ask. Based on the learning style you design for your homeschool, the teaching time can certainly vary.

If you are following a specific curriculum, you'll teach that curriculum for however long it takes. If you're unschooling, then you live a life guided by learning, then teaching can happen at any time (refer to **Method Island** for learning styles).

Let's start with traditional homeschoolers who typically do school at home from 8 am–3 am or 9 am–4 pm, just like traditional school. They usually include recess and lunch breaks, with learning broken up between various subjects. Here, a parent may teach a lesson for 10 or 15 minutes and then have the children complete the work required for another 1/2 hour to 45 minutes.

If we move to the opposite side of the spectrum and look at an unschooler, we'll see no set time for teaching. Instead, learning is happening in every activity in all waking hours. Every day can look different. For example, Andrea has two girls she unschools. After a slow morning watching a couple of shows, the girls gather around the breakfast table and talk about the animals in the show. This leads the oldest, Amber, to pull out her paints and paper to paint a picture of her favorite animal, the hedgehog. The youngest, Abby, asks Andrea to read her a book about the world's weirdest animals. Andrea takes the children on a walk to see if they can find any smaller creatures of the world and compare them to the bigger animals from the show. Abby wants to know why insects and animals are different. Andrea finds a video on YouTube about classifying animals, and the girls watch it intently. They want to learn more and decide to walk to the library to look up various books on insects and animals.

The interest of the girls could last for days, weeks, or even months. Their interest may become a passion, leading to so many other opportunities (think field trips, interviewing scientists or creature experts, museums, botanical gardens, etc.) and a deeper understanding of the subject. There is no timeline for unschoolers. When the children have learned enough about a topic, they will let you know it's time to move on.

These are two very different versions of how long one may teach in a day. However, even a traditional homeschooler doesn't stop at 3 or 4 pm. The curriculum does, but not the constant learning.

How long one teaches definitely varies depending on your style and how you design your homeschool.

How do I get them to learn from others and not just me?

Online classes are a big thing in our house, but you can also look at homeschool co-ops, programs at the library or recreation center, or taking turns teaching with friends.

How do I find other homeschoolers?

Thanks to social media, this has become very easy! You can find a plethora of Facebook groups for homeschoolers – either worldwide or right in your own town, city, state, or province. Even within a city, you can find different types of homeschoolers – from unschoolers to Waldorf-inspired, to traditional.

We can access others in an instant. You could grab your phone and do a quick search now for homeschooling groups in your area. Join a few of their events and see what they have to offer.

Some will have very nominal fees to cover materials for events (like a not-back-to-school picnic!), while others may be free to join.

These groups are where you will find your people. And your children's people. These groups will open you up to other ideas, give you other people to connect with, and become the people that build the village where you raise your children.

Do I need to tell someone I'm homeschooling?

You'll have to look into your local laws to answer this. Every area is different – some require you to notify local authorities, and others require no notifications.

How do I balance school-aged children with a baby who needs my constant attention?

This is the joy of the concept of Homeschool By Design. While you have a baby, things shift and readjust during the time of infant-hood. You design your life around this change, knowing you will redesign things when they are less chaotic.

Chores can be divided by siblings so you can focus on the baby, for example. Perhaps an older sibling can care for the baby while you teach the others. Then they switch, and another sibling steps in to care for the baby. Or maybe the teaching part is done while the baby naps or sits in a carrier on mama's back. Or, even better, perhaps the older child can teach the younger ones – teaching them responsibility and leadership at the same time.

If you have a baby as well as younger children, offer a special activity bin to the younger children as you tend to the baby. Activity bins are the best! I used them when Cruz was born, and Avery was only 1.5 years old and continued to use them well into preschooler age. They can bring so much ease to your day.

Just fill a small bin (hey there, dollar store) with unique items or a simple activity.

Here are a few of the ones I remember creating:

- cleaning supplies for tiny hands, like a hand towel and a plastic spray bottle with water for 'cleaning' the windows or glass door

Avery at 2 years old cleaning the windows with his cloth

- a mini felt board, made from cardboard and a piece of felt glued onto it, along with little felt pieces to tell a story
- pattern sheets and small plastic bear counters in various colors so they could recreate the patterns from the sheet
- a few plastic animals and a toothbrush so the animals could be 'cleaned' (add some water and a squirt of soap to the bin for added fun)

- rice with spoons, funnels, and jars to act as a filling station
- play dishes and a dish towel, filling the bucket with soapy water so they can wash the dishes

Honestly, Pinterest is your best friend here. Just search for 'activity bins' or 'sensory bins' and add their age group. You'll find hundreds of simple ideas right at your fingertips.

I'm pretty certain I shopped exclusively at the dollar store for every one of these items. I feel like I should own stock.

The idea is to have unique items the children won't otherwise see, so it's exciting for them! When you need to focus your attention elsewhere – like to baby – you can use a special bin to keep the younger children occupied until you return.

If you don't have space for multiple bins, keep one bin and switch the activities in it every week.

How do I decide on a curriculum?

Choosing a curriculum is a very personal choice. It's essential to look at the way your children enjoy learning best. Perhaps they love doing worksheets and sitting at the table. Maybe they really enjoy learning through books and reading. Perhaps you love nature as a family and prefer more nature-based learning. Maybe your children are very methodical and would enjoy Montessori related curriculum. Look at the various curriculums available and refer to **Method Island** to get some ideas in your head.

Most companies selling curriculums offer samples. This is the perfect way to see how your children respond to a particular curriculum, theory, or method of education. Try a few different ones for a couple of weeks and see what fits best with them. We have gone the gamut over the years from Waldorf and Montessori-led curriculum to a strictly literature-based curriculum to now where we are using a lot of online platforms. Dabble in many different curriculums as you go along. And here's one little tip: just because you purchased XYZ curriculum doesn't mean you have to stick with it. If it is not right for you or your family, it's okay to let it go. Sell it on a homeschool marketplace and just move on! There's no use trying to push through after one month of unsuccessful mornings and temper tantrums and fights and decide that you'll do this for the next 11 months. Just let it go and move on because you can. This is your Homeschool by Design.

What if my child refuses to read?

I feel for you on this one because I've been here. Avery started to read very early. In fact, I was that mom who purchased the 'teach your baby to read' program. He was literally learning the word 'elephant' by memorizing the letters as symbols at 2 years old. I thought he was brilliant, and I continued to push. Then he stopped. I could do nothing to get this kid to learn to read.

You know what I did? I left it. I understood what it would mean if he were in school and not reading simple phrases and books by grade one, but we were home. The pressure was off.

Instead, I read to him and Cruz every day (and continue to do so into their double-digit ages because it's our favorite part of the day). We would go for walks and point out the names of the streets and read the labels on grocery store items. He didn't realize he was reading, but he was. It just wasn't books, which was fine by me. It took him until he was 9 before he felt comfortable to read books.

When he began to read, I noticed he had trouble telling me what was in the paragraph. If I read him a paragraph, he had no problem reciting it to me. That's when I realized he was more of an auditory learner, just like his daddy! My husband just cannot read a book without having to re-read chapters because he gets distracted and can't remember what was written. Audiobooks? No problem. He remembers them all.

If your child is refusing to read, perhaps consider the learning style they prefer. Do they enjoy listening to you read while they play lego or color in a book? Take this into consideration and adjust as necessary.

Also, remember how all kids can be completely different. While Avery didn't read until he was 9, Cruz was reading those massive 500-page Geronimo Stilton books when he was 6. To each their own and in their own time!

Until what grade can you homeschool?

You can homeschool right through your child's entire education. Many universities have moved some programs online, and you can earn degrees without stepping into a classroom. My boys are years away from university, but if they choose to attend, I imagine most things will be online by then.

How do I not lose myself when I'm with my kids 24/7?

This is a big question and a fear for many. With that, there's lots to remember about the visit to **All About You Island**.

Here's a reminder to the main three ways to not lose yourself:
1. Find hobbies you love and give yourself permission to enjoy them often (without the kids).
2. Set boundaries. It's good for them to see you set boundaries towards themselves and others because you are modeling that behavior.
3. Connect with your friends. We all need adult time when we can let loose and not feel the need to sing 'The Wheels on the Bus.'

What age do I need to start?

This is something to look up for your area. Some countries require every child over the age of six to be educated. Others are early and others later. Most people start to purposefully educate their children at home in the same period they would typically enter the traditional school system. But, honestly, you started as soon as they were born.

Where do I homeschool?

Wherever is best for your kids. For us, it's currently at the kitchen table. It's also been at the 'tinker' table (a smaller table we have for the boys to use for messy crafts and things), the couch, and my bed. You don't need anything fancy. You don't need a separate room or to buy a new house. You can do it in a tiny home, you can do it in an apartment or condo, you can do it in an RV, you can do it in a hotel room (we've done all of these). It doesn't matter where you are. What matters is doing the learning.

Resources – how do I find them?

I know I touched on this already, but Pinterest. Create a Pinterest board dedicated to homeschooling. Or more than one! Homeschooling resources, home-schooling room ideas, homeschooling bloggers, home-schooling schedules, homeschooling documenting, homeschooling curriculum, etc. Instead of spending mindless time scrolling through Facebook or Instagram, scroll through Pinterest for ideas, printables, fun activi-ties, tips, tricks, and resources.

How do I make sure they know what they need to know?

Some parents let their children lead their own learning or use unit studies. Here, you want to docu-ment things well. You want to make notes of the things they ask, research, watch, and do. You can compare that to a general list of 'standards' if you're concerned about their progress.

If you've purchased a set of curriculum, it likely includes tests or assessments. These will keep you on track with your child's learning.

How do you do high school? Can you do it online?

You sure can do it online! Where we live, we can also enroll our kids part-time if they chose to do so.

Look into your local laws and contact your local high school to see if they have options for homeschoolers who may want to take a few classes (like drama, music, or art) at school if that floats your boat. Otherwise, there is plenty of curriculum out there for homeschooling high schoolers. We also have our province's full curriculum available to us if we choose to use it. Check your local resources!

How do I manage my life and theirs *and* my work?

Scheduling. Remember, homeschooling can be done any time. It doesn't have to be done Monday to Friday or September to June. Get a good planner and plan it out, remembering homeschooling only takes a couple of hours a day, depending on the child. You'll notice there's lots of room for your life, their life, your work, *and* their school.

How many hours does it take to plan?

I used to spend HOURS every Sunday planning things and putting things together, but it wasn't working for me. I looked for a better way. If you aren't one for planning every little detail, invest in a solid curriculum package. We *loved* Moving Beyond The Page, which focused entirely on a literature-based curriculum. It was everything in one pack, and we loved it for the years we used it. To really answer this question, it can take hours a week or 20 minutes on a Sunday night. It all depends on whether you're using curriculum and the method of homeschooling you choose.

How do I teach more than one grade at a time?

SCHEDULE! Have older ones help younger ones while you work with another child. Give them independent work times (e.g., one practices piano while the other does computer work while you help the third with math for 20 minutes). Remember (I know I keep saying that ...there's a lot to remember here): you're not homeschooling the entire day. Also, you can combine learning. You can learn about the body systems and have the 6-year-old make a model of the brain from play-dough while the other older ones label parts of the brain. That's a science class for everyone.

How do I teach math when I don't understand it?

Khan Academy – it's free, and they break down every math lesson from preschool to college. You can also look up lessons on YouTube. Plenty of teachers have posted videos explaining fractions and the decimal system. Have no fear – you always have resources right at your fingertips!

How do I make math more fun?

I'll answer a question with a question. What are your kids interested in? Mine love Fortnite, and there are a million ways you can incorporate video gaming into math: games played versus won, elimination per game ratio, fractions for health, and leaderboard statistics. I could go on forever.

You can also find math in baking or cutting a pizza or a cake. Math is everywhere! It's in the weather and the degrees outside. It's in growth charts when we see how much our children have grown. Everywhere!

Think about their most prominent interests and use your Learning Lens to come up with a variety of ways to incorporate the language of math. Just don't call it math when you talk about it, or they will catch on.

How do I socialize them?

Oh, the socialization question! Let me answer it with this simple fact: you will have many places to visit, activities to do, and clubs to attend that you'll actually find it hard *not* to socialize. Socialization opportunities are endless. Unfortunately, this old way of thinking has been passed down to us. It stems from a time before the internet and the ability to meet people in seconds.

Instead of asking how you will socialize your kids, you should *really* ask how you will incorporate all the learning when there's so much socialization going on?!

Now that you know socialization won't be an issue, I hear from many people that the socialization taking part in schools (most especially bullying) is *not* the way they want their children socialized. I guess that's two points awarded to homeschooling.

How do I turn our daily lives into learning opportunities?

Grab your Learning Lens from your satchel and get to it! Just be open and aware of what's going on around you and think of the subjects covered in any particular activity. A walk to the park could include mapping (how to I get from home to the park), reading (street names), and counting (how many streets passed). You probably already do these things, but now your Learning Lens is on, and you're aware. Try doing that for 3 days and see what happens.

How do I know what type of homeschooler we are?

You might not fit just one way, and it might take time before you really know (and does the label matter anyway?). You might find you're more eclectic, picking and choosing a few different versions of homeschooling and making it yours.

How do I write a lesson plan?

If you are lesson planning, it sounds like you are creating all the lessons and resources for your child to learn, which is excellent if you have a passion for it! If it's your thing, keep going! But if this feels heavy or too much, look into a full curriculum or different smaller curriculums to piece together (including art, history, math, writing, grammar, spelling, social studies, science, etc.).

A better idea might be to look at the entire year and what you want to have planned out. Then go into the different months and break those down bit-by-bit. What do you want to cover each month? Are there any holidays you want to focus on? Any breaks you want to take?

Also, you can chunk your learning into blocks instead of covering all the topics at once time. For instance, you might focus on science and math for 3 months, then move onto writing and art for the next 3 months. Later, you'll study history and social studies for 3 months. This offers a more substantial focus on specific subjects at a time.

How do I prepare my kids for post-secondary school?

First, take a peek at the admissions for local universities and colleges. Any of the ones I've looked into have a different process of admissions for homeschoolers. Some even allow high schooled homeschoolers to take a course here and there before officially graduating from high school.

Next, you'll keep detailed records of what they're learning as they go. You want to show progression. Also, document anything required by the universities/colleges your learner intends to consider.

You can keep a transcript for your child based on courses they take online or from the in-hand curriculum. There are a ton of resources out there on how to create these transcripts.

Can I start homeschooling anytime?

Yes, absolutely. If your child has been in school and you decide to pull them out sometime throughout the year, I recommend de-schooling for the first few weeks. Research the benefits of de-schooling and its purpose to determine if it's for you and your child. Basically, the idea behind de-schooling is to allow your child to have a break (I mean, you're pulling them out for a reason, right!?). Also, you'll want to notify the school authorities of your choice and find out if you have any other requirements once you decide to homeschool.

Do I need a teaching degree to homeschool?

Definitely not! Out of all the homeschoolers I know, maybe 1% have some teaching or child-care background. Do you love your kids? Yes. Are you reading this book to find out how you can design the homeschool that fits them and your family best? Yes. That's what you need to be able to homeschool. Love for your kids, an open mind, and the bravery to dive into the homeschooling waters!

Homeschoolers, look at how far you've come in this journey! We have only one more island to visit, and I'm getting a bit hesitant because I don't want this to end. You're far too much of a good travel partner, and I want to keep going. Alas, you do need to start the actual act of homeschooling, so let's travel to our final island.

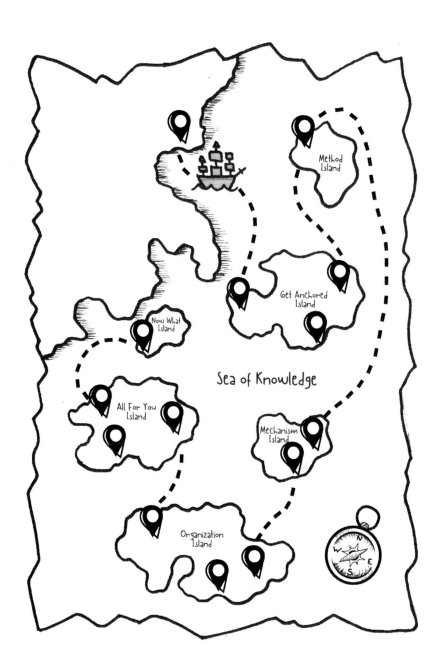

Disembarking from our journey

WE'VE COME TO the end of our quest, my friends! I'm so proud of you! Before we disembark, let's have a quick chat on where to go from here.

Throughout your travels, you completed your Homeschool By Design. You visited all the destinations and gathered all the knowledge you will need once you disembark. Your Field Guide is complete, a precious treasure you hold in your hand. Refer to it often, lean on it for support, and change it when needed.

Use the imaginary tools from your satchel as often as you need them (the Learning Lens will be your best ally).

Take a moment to look back at your progress. You battled every pirate – like tackling the comparison thief. You overcame every obstacle – like how to organize your homeschool. You built your belief in being able to do this – by changing your thoughts. Be proud of yourself. You are ready to start homeschooling. The real deal, it's time!

Before we do our goodbye hugs, let me give you a few last tips about starting your homeschool year:

1. Start a tradition for your first day of homeschooling. It could be something small, like getting donuts at your favorite donut shop or lunch at your favorite restaurant, or it can be something big like a full-day field trip. Let this tradition continue annually on the first day of every new homeschool year.

2. Go slowly at first. Try not to throw all the curriculum at your kids at once. Take the first few weeks to gradually introduce each topic/subject and let everyone in the house get used to homeschooling slowly and thoughtfully.

3. You'll get stuck in a rut. It doesn't happen right away, but within a few weeks or months, you'll see the excitement starts to fade. I'm not telling you this to scare you, but to let you know, it's normal. Don't let it discourage you! Just find ways to spice things up when it feels like you're stuck at sea with no wind at your back. Take a break, move items around, or introduce something different for a week.

4. Your house will be messy. And that's ok.

5. Love every moment – even the fighting ones. You've been gifted the most magical experience and will look back on these years when you're old and grey with a heart filled with gratitude. You won't remember the hard times, like when Kylie scratched her brother so hard that he bled or when the window was left open, and you yelled at your toddler so

loud that the neighbors looked over and shook their heads at you. Those memories won't last. The good ones will.

You made it safely back and have the work to prove your adventure. Although this is the end of the book, it's just the beginning of the next step of your homeschool journey. Join us online at HomeschoolBy-Design.com or the Facebook group Homeschool By Design for support as you navigate new waters.

It's been an honor to travel these pages with you. Know that I believe in you and that you absolutely can do this. Go forward now and live your Homeschool By Design!

BONUS CHAPTER

Educating during a quarantine

YOU DIDN'T NOTICE it, but just off our map is the rarely-visited **Quarantine Island.** At the time of this writing we are knee-deep in the pandemic, and still in partial quarantine where I live. So I included this bonus island to visit. Hooray!

The pandemic is actually the reason I pushed so hard to finish this book. The number of parents coming to me for support, hearts hurting with frustration as their children try to navigate online learning with tears, was many. They all had the same questions, trying to navigate these new waters they've been tossed into. And without a guide, nonetheless!

This book was screaming to be written. It needed its ideas on paper. It needed to reach more people than I could reach in a day. It's been an honor to be chosen to write it, and I sit excitedly on my chair imagining the families this will support who are dealing with homeschooling the same way all of us are – through crisis-schooling.

The term 'crisis-schooling' was coined recently, and I agree with this term because we certainly aren't homeschooling. Homeschooling looks nothing like this.

There are no hikes, no field trips, no time with friends, no museum or library visits, no picnics, no finding shells and sea glass at the beach and spending the day researching them, no road trips leading to a discovery of a new place, no days hopping in the car and seeing where our day will lead.

Stuck at home 24/7 is not homeschooling, and I want you to be reminded this can be hard for some (if not all). So, if you're struggling right now, remember you're not alone, and this isn't what homeschooling is like. However, it's still a time that can lead to learning if you'd like it to be.

Rules for Teaching at Home (even for a season)

1. It never needs to 'look' like school. I mean, it can if you're the type that needs structure. But it doesn't have to. We slant more towards the relaxed home-schooling method because our boys thrive in that environment, so our days look nothing close to a 'typical' school day. And neither ways are right or wrong.

2. Life is school. Even the mail carrier has important things to teach your kids.

3. A day of building pirate ships in Minecraft is a successful day (imagination, architecture, the science of the ocean, buoyancy, design, history of pirates and their ships, perimeter, area....I can go on and on)

4. Baking. And more baking.

5. Just because they're having fun doesn't mean they aren't learning. In fact, it means they're learning and absorbing that much more.

6. It takes nowhere near the same time to teach your kids as the number of hours they are in school. Remember: you don't have interruptions, recess, breaks, or lines of kids needing help like a classroom has. You have only your kids.

7. You 100% don't have to be a teacher to teach your kids. You don't need to know algebra or have the periodic table memorized. The joy lies in learning *with* your kids. If you love them and want what's best for them, you are more than qualified to teach them, even for a day.

8. You can, in fact, spend the day in your PJs. Or three days.

Keep Up with Expectations

Articles on this are now in the thousands. If you decide to homeschool during the pandemic – I'm talking throwing distance learning out the window and going on your own here – the expectation is to keep everyone healthy and happy.

If you are only choosing to homeschool during the closures, enjoy the time with your kids by doing activities that inspire you and them. Let go of the added pressure of meeting certain expectations. Give yourself some grace.

This time has been compared to that of war times in the first half of the 20th century. During times like these, survival is most important. Families have come together during this time and gathered more appreciation for the things we usually take for granted, like playing at the park.

Expectations in our family during this time are to keep everyone's mental wellness at the forefront. Learning won't stop – kids are naturally curious beings. And teachers will be spending lots of time reviewing concepts once schools go back to 'normal.'

North American expectations are set high, typically. But this isn't a typical time. Instead of the hustle and bustle of our society, we're forced to slow down (finally), so embrace it!

Socialization

I am very lenient during this time of the quarantine when it comes to playing video games because it's the only time they get to 'see' their friends and socialize. Although this might not work for every child/parent/family, it's what works for us. And it's been amazing. They learn communication skills, leadership (although Avery can be quite the 'leader' when it comes to this...a skill we talk about over dinner: 'how can we let our friends call the shots, too'), strategy, math, all sorts of good stuff!

You can also download the app Houseparty and get friends to join in fun games like Heads Up, trivia, and Quick Draw. They can hop on Facetime or Zoom with their friends for quick chats. I've even seen birthday parties held on Zoom, complete with fun party games for all the kids to enjoy for an hour.

<u>Working from Home During the Pandemic</u>

If you remember from **All About You Island**, we set reasonable expectations when working and homeschooling. I want you to lower those expectations. We are in a pandemic, and our goal here is to have our kids look back on this and remember how awesome it was they got to do XYZ and how their family wasn't chaotic. Aim for those memories over the frantic parent struggling to balance it all.

Also, I know we've heard it a million times, but we really are all in this together. I'm sure those people you're on a virtual call with are *also* at home and *also* have kids asking for a granola bar. We all understand each other and can give each other some grace when the kid comes in the room in the middle of your call, asking you to look at their poop.

<u>Subject Ideas</u>

Here's a run-down of some of the things we've enjoyed as a family during this stay-in-place order.

Art

- Art For Kids Hub on YouTube. I told you about him in this quest already, but this amazing father teaches us how to draw as he teaches his own children. All in such a supportive and loving way. It's awesome! And he has all sorts of video game characters, emojis, holiday themes and more.

Music

- Just YouTube what you want! Avery initially taught himself how to play the ukulele from a wonderful woman on YouTube.

- Have a dance party.

- Take the beat of a fav song and see if you can replicate it by ear on a piano. Don't have a piano? Download a piano app.

- Play different types of music and ask the kids to dance the way it makes them feel. From classical to EDM, this makes for a fun game and ridiculous movements.

- Download Garage Band, where they can produce their own music. This has inspired the boys to have their own DJ names and social media handles where they share their music.

Yoga & Meditation

- Cosmic Kids Yoga on YouTube. Jamie brings so much fun to yoga with every theme imaginable – from Harry Potter to Frozen. Great for so many ages!

- The Headspace app. We end every night with a meditation with Daddy from Headspace. They have more than enough free meditations to calm at bedtime. Use Lavender on the pillows for the more rambunctious ones.

Confidence and Growth Mindset

- Check out the Big Life Journal website. If nothing else, grab their freebies and sign up for their news-letter. You'll get growth mindset activities for your kids every week. Oh, how the world would be so different if all the kids were confident in who they are here to be!

Writing

- Daily gratitude journals

- Freewriting: They pull a topic from a jar and write as much or as little as they like. Don't judge for grammar or spelling. Rejoice in whatever creation they come up with – confidence in their writing is key here!

- At the end of the day, have them write out what they loved best or how they were a good sibling.

Foreign Language

- You must download DuoLingo Kids. It teaches French or Spanish for free in a fun way that they'll want to learn! While you're at it, download it for yourself, too. I'm learning Spanish.

Science

- Operation Ouch on YouTube. I've told you about these twin brothers, but they are worth mentioning again here. They are doctors and cover an incredible amount of info about the human body. We love their funny videos and learn so much. The boys especially love the gross experiments. Obvi.

- Earth Rangers podcast and app. Getting this free membership will truly inspire your kids to take action when it comes to saving animals and our planet!

- Take a walk outside. Bake cookies. Make bread rise. There's science everywhere.

Reading

- Allow them to stay up as late as they want if they're reading a good book.

- Snuggle up on the couch with some tea and read them a chapter book – a few chapters each day to keep them captivated. Pick something with adventure and mystery!

- Grab a book of silly poems and participate in some Poetry TeaTime. Ours has become so successful that our neighborhood friends pop in to join us (when not in quarantine)!

Math

- Check out the Khan Academy website. If you've never been to this site....prepare for your mind to be blown. You could literally have access to only this site, and your kid would be forever educated. From math to science, history to grammar, computers to personal finance, this site covers everything for every single grade, all for free. The world has access to free education and doesn't even know it! Take advantage!

<u>When the Going Gets Rough</u>

We had a rough week recently, and I had to switch things up for my boys. You can do this, too, whether you need a mental wellness break, a nap, or a coffee alone in bed while watching your favorite show. Note they are nine and eleven, so it may not be do-able for younger kiddies, but that's what Wild Kratts is for (do kids still watch that show?!).

1. I taught them how to take notes (on their iPads, but it can be on paper, journal, computer, etc.).
2. I had them write a list of 30 things they loved to do (hard at first, but we wrote down every board game, video game, fav TV show, as well as things like cooking, photography, magic, etc.).
3. From that list, I asked them to pick one thing and do that thing while documenting it. And if they got bored, find something else on their list to do.

I basically outsourced the documenting of learning (remember **Mechanism Island?**) to my kids.

Here's what they did from those instructions:

- Played multiple rounds of Fortnite, documented all their eliminations, made notes on what they could have done better in that round
- Watched a documentary on the Knights Templar and made notes about the cool technology used to find things underground (which led to more research into these technologies in the following days)
- Watched all the Fortnite Live Events on YouTube and documented each of the dates, what took place, which season it was in, and how he felt about each one (like, you know, which one was coolest)

- Used a big box to create a box fort: noting the steps to create it with photos

Even in the craziness of not being able to leave our homes (now I know how animals in zoos feel) and even when we just can't do it anymore, this is still a time that can lead to lots of learning. If you want it to.

It was a quick visit to **Quarantine Island**, but take with you these essential souvenirs:

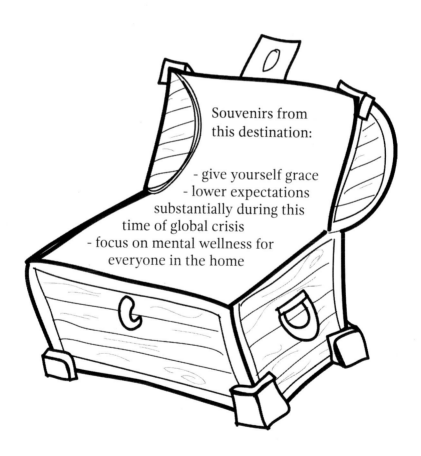

Souvenirs from this destination:

- give yourself grace
- lower expectations substantially during this time of global crisis
- focus on mental wellness for everyone in the home

NOTES

NOTES

Acknowledgements

Many people deserve a big hug.

I want to start off by thanking YOU for choosing this book. It was meant for you and written for you. I know this because the book flowed through me. It needed to be written because it knew you needed it.

I also want to thank some key people who helped make this all happen.

Thank you to Sage Adderley-Knox, who held me accountable to my goals and guided me through every step. You kept my futuristic brain in the present and calmed my fears of putting this out there. You are amazing!

Thank you to my beta readers: Eileen Lee (my mom!), Angela Martin, Christina Silveira, and Steph Collins. Your honest feedback and thorough reading helped bring the concept to life!

Angela Martin, an extra thank you to you as we walked the writing path together, daily. You celebrated every step with enthusiasm and love and continued to keep me excited. You remind me of the possibilities we all have - you are the greatest friend!

To Louie - you are my rock! Despite the enormous things you are doing in this world, you spend all the time listening to me babble about our homeschool day, about my progress for this book, and figuring out why my website doesn't look just so. You are the love of my life, and this journey of homeschooling (and life) is SO much more fun with you next to me.

To my boys - one day, I hope you'll read this and think of all the fun we've had together. We've designed our entire lives perfectly for you so you can thrive. I cannot wait to see how you design your own lives one day and show up in the world as only you can!

To the cacao harvesters - thank you. Chocolate is my life.

ABOUT MONICA

Monica is a serial entrepreneur with a huge passion for teaching. She has been a home-educating mama since 2009.

Obsessed with traveling, Monica and her family of four can be found exploring North America a quarter of the year. Following the mantra *life by design*, both she and her husband have built businesses that allow them to travel often. As a family, they have experienced more than half the US states, half the Canadian provinces, and six countries, learning the whole time.

When not traveling, Monica can be found writing, studying her ancestry, and eating vegan chocolate. Not necessarily in that order.

Recently featured on a national TV station with multiple segments on the transition to homeschooling, Monica has a Facebook group she uses to support hundreds of families as they educate their children from home.

Besides homeschooling, Monica is the founder of one of Canada's biggest vegan food festivals, an essential oils educator, speaker, and author.